TWENTY JOBS TWENTY LESSONS

a long, strange career in marketing,
from junk mail to social media

by BOB CARGILL

TWENTY JOBS, TWENTY LESSONS — A LONG, STRANGE CAREER IN MARKETING, FROM JUNK MAIL TO SOCIAL MEDIA

Author: Cargill, Bob
Publication Date: June 2022
Publisher: Bob Cargill's Marketing Show
Visit Bob's Website: thebobcargill.com
Book Format: Print
ISBN 978-0-578-38190-9

This book has been written as a memoir. It is a reflection and encapsulation of what the author, Bob Cargill, remembers at this time about his career so far. Some names have been changed. Some descriptions and dialogue may have been slightly reimagined to protect the privacy of others.

THANK YOU

Thank you to my wife, Barbara, for being so patient with me while I have sat in front of my computer all these hours, day in and day out, working on this book. The appreciation I have for your love and unconditional support cannot be overstated.

Thank you to my two sons, Scott and Ben, for putting up with me talking about this book for well over three years, saying I'm almost done with it, I'm almost done with it. Hey boys, I'm now — finally — done with it.

Thank you to my editor, Morgan Hume, and book designer, Maria Antonia Silva, for your ridiculously awesome talent and dedication to seeing this book through with me.

Thank you to Deborah Hepburn, a teacher I had back in the day at Franklin High School who encouraged me to keep a journal, something I did for quite a few years back in the day, instilling in me a passion for sharing my story with as many people as possible.

Thank you to David Hazeltine, who gave me the green light on my idea of starting a blog in 2004 at his company and gave me permission to take that blog with me in perpetuity. I will always be grateful for your support and generosity, David.

Thank you to all my amazing colleagues and friends who I have been blessed to have worked alongside of all these years.

And finally, thank you to all my former employers and bosses for the many great opportunities you gave me to work for you and develop my skills, not to mention to enjoy a super solid career in the marketing, advertising and social media industries.

Bob Cargill
June 1, 2022

This book starts with me driving an ice cream truck and ends with me driving for a large, well-known ride-sharing company. I didn't do either for very long, but both part-time jobs taught me the importance of hard work, hustle, customer service, street smarts and patience.

In between, I've focused on the full-time jobs that had the most to do with my career in marketing so far.

I hope you enjoy reading this book. It's not just my story. It could be your story, too, of trying to climb the corporate ladder only to fall down time and time again, seeking the perfect job situation and trying to conquer the world — that is, the corporate world.

I've learned most of my lessons the hard way, and I hope to share those lessons with you so you know what I didn't know at the time I made my own mistakes.

You'll step back in time with me for a little while, but you'll also be taken along my long, strange career journey from junk mail to social media, all the way up to just a few years ago. Thanks for coming along for the ride.

This book that I have been working on since the beginning of 2019 is a chronicle of my career in marketing so far, having worked at over a dozen different agencies — as a copywriter, creative director, and other such titles — in addition to a few large companies.

This is a story about climbing up the corporate ladder only to fall down time and time again.

This is a story for anybody involved in the fields of marketing, advertising, PR and social media.

This is a story about business. This is a story about ambition. This is a story about resolve. This is a story about frustration.

This is a story for young professionals with bright futures in front of them and senior executives who have been there and done that.

This is a story about how marketing has changed in the last four decades and how one creative professional has kept his eyes on the prize despite the moving target.

DEAR READER,

First of all, thank you so very, very much for your interest in reading my book. I could not be more appreciative of your time, support and friendship.

This book starts with one part-time summer job I had as a teenager and then covers every full-time corporate job in the marketing industry I had from 1983 until early 2017. You'll find a small variety of pictures to look at about halfway through the book. It ends with me driving around the Boston area for another part-time job for a large, well-known ride-sharing company.

Beginning with Job 14, I have included some of the blog posts from the blog I started in 2004 for you to read. Concurrent with the recap of my full-time job experiences, these posts will chronicle the emergence and evolution of social media from my perspective.

I hope you enjoy reading about my long, strange career.

I hope you enjoy reading my book.

Bob Cargill

TABLE OF CONTENTS

INTRODUCTION

I don't know what has been more exciting...

__ Traveling to New York City, Chicago and Los Angeles to teach seminars about direct mail back in the day or being flown out to the midwest for a big job interview — which I nailed — early in my career.

Partnering up with some of the most talented agency principals in Massachusetts to help bring in new business or managing a team of ridiculously awesome creative professionals — copywriters, designers, and art directors — to get the resultant work done.

Writing all those articles on social media for ClickZ from 2014-2017 or writing all those posts on social media and marketing for my blog since its inception in 2004.

Serving as president of the New England Direct Marketing Association for the fiscal year 1999-2000 or serving as president of the American Marketing Association Boston for the fiscal years 2018-2020.

Recording hundreds of videos about marketing and social media on my own YouTube channel or interviewing dozens of amazing guests for my own podcast about the same topics.

There were the first two jobs I had out of graduate school when I worked — back-to-back — in high-rise buildings in Manhattan at two of the biggest music companies in the world.

Or there was the seven-year run I had as the owner of my own business in the '90s during which time I won a handful of awards for my work — including the top award, Best of Show, at the New England Direct Marketing Shoestring Awards Show in 1994 — and for a while even had an office in Faneuil Hall Marketplace in Boston.

There was another award I received from the New England Direct Marketing Association in 2009, the Direct Marketer of the Year award.

There is all the teaching I have been doing as an adjunct professor of marketing and social media at several universities in Boston since I left the full-time corporate world in the spring of 2017. I can't tell you how happy I am doing what I am doing today.

All that said, it may appear that I've led a charmed career. Right? But that has been far from the case. My career up to this point has been a long, strange series of ups and downs, fits and starts, successes, yes, but also plenty of failures. It hasn't been an easy career, but it has certainly been an exciting career. There has never been a dull moment in all the days of my professional life. I have had some outstanding bosses, mentors and clients. I have made some lifelong friends. I have had some incredible experiences. I have learned some important lessons.

I have been extremely lucky to have made a living getting paid to do something I love to do, communicating with as many people as possible as effectively as possible on behalf of others.

LESSON 1
DO THE RIGHT THING

LESSON 1, DO THE RIGHT THING
WHATEVER YOU DO ON THE JOB, ALWAYS CONSIDER THE EFFECT YOUR ACTIONS WILL HAVE ON YOUR CLIENTS, COLLEAGUES AND CUSTOMERS. TAKE YOUR ROLE AND RESPONSIBILITIES SERIOUSLY. BE KIND, RESPECTFUL, DUTIFUL AND LOYAL. A GOOD WORK ETHIC GOES A LONG WAY TOWARDS THE DEVELOPMENT OF A SUCCESSFUL CAREER.

Circa 1978

As many jobs I have had during the course of my career so far, I worked at almost as many prior — maybe more — to becoming a marketing professional. I did everything from working at a dog kennel where I fed the dogs and cleaned their runs, to pumping gas at not just one, but two Mobil gas stations in Massachusetts — one in Franklin, the town in which I grew up, the other in Amherst, while I was going to school at UMass Amherst.

I delivered flowers and newspapers. I worked at a liquor store, a convenience store and a department store. I cleaned condominiums and car dealerships. I loaded trucks. I mowed lawns. I painted houses.

However, one of the most interesting part-time jobs I had back in the day was driving an ice cream truck for a short while in my hometown.

I may not have driven that truck for long, but it was still a job I'll never forget. This wasn't just any ice cream truck. This was an old, third-rate ice cream truck that I was almost too embarrassed about to drive. Looking back, I think of it as a unique job that I should be proud of, but I think I was a little mortified to find myself driving around my stomping grounds selling frozen confections and treats out of a big, old white truck that blasted an old, cheesy jingle to alert the neighborhood of my arrival.

It was the truck. It was the song. It was the ice cream. None of it was cool at a time in my life when everything I did publicly needed to be cool. It was the complete opposite of the impression I wanted to give even complete strangers, never mind if any of my friends in town happened to see me.

Not that I didn't like driving the truck. It was just being seen doing so.

And I learned a lot. I got the job from a friend of my dad's. This gentleman was a painter and this was a side gig of his. I gave it my all, but only for a short time.

I learned that without a good audience, people who are interested in what you have to offer, it doesn't matter how good your products and services are, you will fail.

For some reason, I was never that busy. I drove around town and stopped when I saw customers waiting for me. Mostly kids. Some families. A few teenagers.

The pay was less than par. At the end of my shift, I would drop the day's earnings onto my boss's dining room table, with me getting a share of the proceeds. He'd sometimes give me a beer — a welcome bonus, especially for a teenager, albeit one of legal drinking age, mind you — while we counted the money.

I'm happy I had the gig. It certainly was a unique opportunity. I'm sorry I didn't give any notice when I decided I couldn't do the job anymore. My boss was very disappointed, and let my dad know that I should have given him at least two weeks' warning. Not the proudest moment of my professional life. Quite the contrary. But a good lesson learned by bumping my head, figuratively speaking.

The marketing lesson learned was that no matter what business you're in, you need to be where your customers are, and you can signal that presence with music — or a catchy phrase, a loud noise, a unique mascot, etc. — like an ice cream truck arriving on the scene out of the blue. If that music isn't what they want to hear, or even worse, if there is nobody even there to hear it, you are going to be at a loss. Plain and simple.

An even more important life lesson learned was that some jobs aren't what they're cracked up to be, but even if your job sucks, suck it up, hang in there as long as possible and give at least two weeks' notice before you leave. It's the right thing to do. And besides, you don't want to burn any bridges.

You want to be respectful to your employer and do the right thing. My boss, was a really nice guy, and to this day I am sorry to have let him down.

LESSON 2

PLAY THE PART

LESSON 2, PLAY THE PART

EARLY IN YOUR CAREER, TRY TO FIND COLLEAGUES AND MENTORS WHO YOU CAN TRUST AND EMULATE. LEARN FROM THEM. FOLLOW THEIR LEAD. ROOKIE MISTAKES ARE EASY TO MAKE WHEN YOU'RE DOING THINGS FOR THE FIRST TIME.

1983-1984

You might say I was on the verge of adulthood. I was about to graduate with a master's degree in television from Brooklyn College, sprung on the working world like a caged lion set free.

I wanted to go into broadcasting, but I had done a lot of freelance writing in my college days, especially at UMass Amherst, where I earned my B.A. degree in both Communication Studies and English. I had some real-world experience in that field already, so to say I was ambitious would be an understatement.

I applied for jobs in television and radio, doing what was expected of me, but I also considered the possibility that I could become a professional writer. I had written plenty of movie, concert and album reviews for several small newspapers. I was confident I had the chops. I could see myself plying my craft at one of those major publications — like Rolling Stone, Variety or The Village Voice.

I saw a classified ad for a direct response copywriter job. Of course, I was somewhat clueless as to how to interpret the job description, but it mentioned writing about music for this huge, well-known company in Manhattan.

I applied immediately. Like I did for all the other jobs I was pursuing, I cut out the ad, taped it to an index card and tucked it away in the small, yellow plastic recipe box I was using to organize my job search.

Before long that job was mine and the rest, as they say, is history. My career as a copywriter in the marketing field was launched.

I wrote promotional blurbs about popular music for this company's record and tape club — you know, vinyl, which has made quite a comeback lately, as well as cassettes and 8-track tapes. Can you believe it? I couldn't. I had my own office not just with a door, but with a stereo system. My job was to listen to music and write about it for a catalog that went out to millions of people of all ages who would use it to shop for the hippest sounds and latest tunes.

Negative option. That was the strategy. Members had the option to say no to receiving the music we selected for them each month. If they returned a card in the mail declining the shipment, they were off the hook. But if they ignored that card, whether intentionally or not, they were mailed music for which they owed a tidy sum.

Negative option. A strategy that resulted in a cash cow the likes of which not just this company, but countless other direct marketing operations were lucky to have seen back in those heady days of mail order.

To this day, I remember being taken out for my first business lunch as an employee. My boss took me to Sardi's in Times Square. Yes, that Sardi's, where famous caricatures of show business stars dot the walls and you may even find yourself in the company of one or two of them. Don't tell me I wasn't being set up for disappointment later on in my career. Talk about starting at the top. I was spoiled rotten at that job and I didn't even know it.

What I was doing on this job was classic, timeless direct response advertising. Master this stuff and you had the chops to go almost anywhere in the field. I worked hard, but how hard could it be to type away to the sounds of Pat Benatar, Kenny Rogers, Def Leppard, Rick Springfield, Menudo, Michael Jackson and Madonna?

This was adulting to me before that even was a thing. I was commuting in from Park Slope on the 3 Train, reading the Times and the tabloids, wearing dark aviator sunglasses, carrying a briefcase and listening to a dance tunes and rock music on my Sony Walkman.

After work, I was shopping at Macy's, Gimbels and even Brooks Brothers, as I was wearing a tie every day, sometimes even a coat and tie.

I took pride in my professional appearance and did my best to act the part, too.

"Hi, this is Robert Cargill," I would answer the phone at my desk, patiently waiting for two or three rings so as not to appear too eager as a rookie to take calls.

Robert was how people addressed me at the time, not Bob. For some reason, that was what I had decided to go by my first few years in the workforce, and the only time in my life. Maybe that was it. My moniker was more formal. What about Bob? Who cares? But Robert, now he was someone worthy of attention.

My role model was Alexander, the first designer I ever worked with in my career, someone I looked up to and made sure to emulate.

Alexander was smooth. Alexander was sophisticated. He was polished where I was rough, confident where I was hesitant.

We worked together on many different projects while I was there, and I always knew I could count on him to make me look good. He was loyal, trustworthy and kind. He was someone who always had your back, which was something I didn't realize was so rare in a business environment until I learned the hard way later on in my career.

He was only one of a small handful of designers I worked with, though, each of whom accorded me respect the likes of which I had rarely seen in my life. So this is what it's like to work in a high-falutin professional office environment, I thought to myself. I can get used to this.

"Can you get it to me by Thursday?" I might be asked by any one of them. "Can you edit your copy down to 200 characters?" one of the others might ask. I was being treated with deference and being given the benefit of the doubt. I was being treated like a professional when I had only been a student less than a year ago. Writing on my electric typewriter — an IBM Selectric, perhaps, state-of-the-art equipment — I took great pains not to make any mistakes. Not just because I didn't want to be corrected by my superiors, but otherwise I would have to use this stuff called White-Out — which was like paint, but sticky, messy and time-consuming — to cover up my own errors before typing over them.

I know, it was like the dark ages.

I had not just one, but three different bosses during my time at this company, each of whom were at the top of their game when it came to direct marketing. I was fortunate to be learning from the best. They were like characters on the show, Mad Men. Straight out of central casting, only I didn't know it at the time. They were smart, sharp, savvy, sophisticated and willing to take me under their wings. There were plenty of deadlines, but nothing as tight as those I would be dealing with in jobs to come. Revisions were few, too.

I was a lucky young man. I couldn't have had a better first job out of grad school.

Plus, did I mention the free records? Every few weeks or so, huge stacks of vinyl would be placed out in the hallway and once word got out, almost everyone would emerge from their offices like kids in a candy store hoping to get their hands on their fair share of this swag.

There's a reason I was able to amass a collection of some 2,000 albums, all of which I still have — collecting dust and mildew in my cellar — to this day.

I had nothing to complain about at this job.

Yet I do remember being so frustrated once that I stormed out of my office, angered perhaps by having to make yet another edit to my copy, and throwing a pen down the corridor only to see the president of the entire company coming around the corner at the same time. Thankfully, he was forgiving.

Overall, though, this job was almost too good to believe. At an office party one night, I was having so much fun that I wound up dancing on one of the desks in the office to some of those tunes I wrote about during the day.

I may have worked hard, but I played hard, too.

All good things had to come to an end, though. I told you I was ambitious. I have never been one to let the grass grow under my feet.

Working there was certainly an auspicious start to my career, but I was anxious to climb the corporate ladder.

I interviewed at one of the biggest sweepstakes companies, known for their catchphrase "you might already be a millionaire," but for some reason that didn't pan out.

And then there was that sweet opportunity at a big, fancy ad agency in the city. If I got this job, my career path would have taken a different direction. They were looking for an account executive, a suit as opposed to a creative guy like me, but they had me in for an interview just the same.

Whether I aced the interview or not, despite how meticulous I was about my wardrobe, I apparently wasn't dressed for the part. I committed a fashion faux pas. I wore cowboy boots. No, not actually cowboy boots, but boots. You know, dress boots. Not tie shoes. Not Oxfords. Boots. Boots that certainly weren't made for walking into a job interview at this company. No, not the best way to make a good first impression.

"You can't wear boots to an interview for an account executive job," one of my colleagues told me after the fact. "They want you to look a certain way."

In a word, a suit. That's how some in the industry commonly referred to those who worked on the business side of things (versus those on the creative side like me).

Those boots ensured my career would continue as someone who earned his livelihood actually making the product, not selling it.

Those boots led to my being a clotheshorse on the job, though, if I wasn't one already, dressing for success from head to, yes, toe.

Those boots resulted in an inadvertent turning point in my career, a fateful experience.

As was my move to another huge music-related company in the city, where I eventually landed a new job as an Advertising Manager.

I was climbing the corporate ladder, as they say, in the business world already. I was feeling my oats maybe a little too soon.

LESSON 3

NOT SO FAST

LESSON 3, NOT SO FAST

GIVE YOURSELF TIME TO SETTLE INTO A NEW JOB. ROLL WITH THE CHANGES AND CHALLENGES. DON'T BE TOO QUICK TO GIVE UP WHEN THINGS AREN'T GOING YOUR WAY. PATIENCE IS A VIRTUE.

1984-1985

So, yes, I did it. I jumped ship. There was hardly any difference in my commute into the city, though. I went from the 3 train to the F train, from one tall building on the Avenue of the Americas to another in Rockefeller Center.

But I was climbing the corporate ladder — literally — to a window office high up in 75 Rockefeller Plaza (75 Rock), a recognizable, iconic skyscraper if ever there was one at a very prestigious address.

I couldn't have loved any more the feeling I had every morning walking to work. I was walking on cloud nine, never mind the busy, bustling streets of midtown Manhattan.

On my way into the office, I would see Radio City Music Hall, the NBC building at 30 Rockefeller Plaza (30 Rock) — home of Saturday Night Live, then and to this day — and the famous ice skating rink near where they erect that equally recognizable Christmas tree every year.

I was walking by all the fancy people in their fancy clothes and feeling like I was fancy just like them.

I thought I would never work anywhere else for the rest of my career. This was it. I had arrived. I had seen my future, and it was in a corner office in a magnificent building in a big city that never sleeps.

Little did I know what the future had in store for me.

I had my own administrative assistant in my second job out of graduate school, the only time in my career I ever had one.

Her name was Bernadette.

She gave me a coffee mug that said, "No More Mister Nice Guy." She thought I was too nice to survive in the business world, which I was already learning could be cold, harsh and ruthless.

She was very, very supportive of me, and helped reinforce my rapidly increasing sense of self-importance.

I became so full of myself that I wrote a long memo to my boss suggesting that our entire advertising strategy, which I had just inherited in the last month or two, (not to mention that I was only two years into my career), was out of line and antiquated.

And I had it distributed to all the corporate types. Can you believe it?

My boss, Al, appeared in the door to my office, holding that infamous memo in his hand and asking with incredulousness (understandably so), "Why did you write this memo?"

It was my Jerry Maguire manifesto before there even was a Jerry Maguire movie, only I was a relative nobody. I was a legend in my own mind, I suppose, but obviously not a movie star. It was the beginning of my swan song there, whether I knew it then or not.

To some degree, I was flying blind, sure, but I was succeeding in my own inimitable way despite myself.

I had pretty good instincts, generally, and I knew I could write.

I was very professional, carrying myself well in conversations and in meetings, even though I never liked "playing office."

I learned at an early age the importance of building solid relationships with people, so getting along with others in the workplace was never a problem.

In fact, I was often too nice to people. At least that's what Bernadette thought. Remember?

One day, a meeting had been arranged for me with another company somewhere on the other side of the Hudson River in New Jersey, which to me could have been on the other side of the world.

Of course, I missed my train and arrived unfashionably late. I was embarrassed and apologetic, but it was impossible to make up for the poor impression I had made on our business partners.

This was the work life of Reilly, though, compared to what the bulk of my career in the future would resemble. I worked out in the company gym, ate lunch in the cafeteria and held court in my office with Bernadette and a small team of supporters.

For a couple years after graduate school, I was batting 1,000. I was working back-to-back at two music industry behemoths, company names you would recognize, in the heart of the Big Apple.

I loved New York — the pace, the lights, the noise, the people. What wasn't there to like about being a young, single, ambitious and upwardly mobile white-collar professional?

But then *this* happened.

"We're relocating to Secaucus, New Jersey," I was told. Wait! What? Just when I thought it was safe to take my foot off the gas pedal and put my career on cruise control.

Some people were refusing to go, Bernadette among them, but I felt I had no choice. I couldn't abandon ship yet.

All the managers were getting company cars except me. I didn't own a car. I would have to soon. I didn't want to go. This was the last thing I would have expected.

My dream of working in the city had been unceremoniously dashed. This was a nightmare.

I should have known it was too good to last. Only a few months into a job that I had taken in part for the prestige and the status, I went from feeling like I had it made in Manhattan to knowing I was going to be reverse-commuting from Park Slope in Brooklyn to a big, old warehouse in another state.

That was the beginning of the end of my dream of working in the city. That was the interruption in my career I never saw coming and certainly had no idea how to handle.

My parents came through for me. I had recently sold my cool, red 1974 Ford Mustang, so they sold me their red — not quite so cool — Ford Fiesta. The price was a bargain and the racing stripe on the car was a bonus. I was back in the saddle.

I hired Samantha as a new assistant. Given this was her home state, she helped me to get acclimated to my new digs in the industrial park near the former slaughterhouse in the middle of basically nowhere.

I took advantage of a second wind and poured myself into the job of promoting sheet music and song books. I conducted meetings, managed a budget, worked with designers and mentored team members.

I grew frustrated with the interminably, long commute, though, and relatively quickly decided I needed to find a job back in the city.

I was growing up fast in the business world, realizing what I could and couldn't do, as well as learning firsthand what I liked and didn't like about business.

I gained experience collaborating with designers and managing projects, not to mention teams. I continued to work hard for long hours, setting a tone and establishing a routine that would last me to this day.

Frankly, I glamorized work, putting senior-level executives on pedestals despite their obvious shortcomings, imperfections and outright failings.

I aspired to be as powerful, wealthy and as smooth as them, to climb the same corporate ladder, to follow in their footsteps, minus their deficiencies, shortcomings and imperfections.

But I quickly grew tired of that drive to and from work — from Park Slope to Secaucus, over bridges and through tunnels — and began looking for another job back in the city.

It didn't take me very long before I was interviewed for a great gig (thanks to a very personal, custom direct mail piece I had written on spec that was personally addressed to my future boss), only they were offering me an even better opportunity if I were to head to the Midwest, not midtown.

Okay. So, I jumped at the opportunity, prematurely to say the least. I was flown out to Des Moines, Iowa, to interview at a large, successful publishing company for a great senior-level copywriting job. My future boss, Cindy, and her husband, Fred, took me sailing, treating me to wine and cheese, and a refreshingly good time.

I was headstrong and impressionable, vulnerable to such courting.

I sold them on my direct mail copywriting prowess and they played up America's heartland. I somehow won them over with my talent and charm in return for a trip to the land of corn dogs and flat lands.

The fact that I took my time in relocating out there should have been enough of an omen to me. I was supposed to start on a Monday, yet I didn't even arrive in the capital of Iowa till Thursday of that week.

Idealistic, young me thought very little of being tardy, though. You'd think I would have already had learned my lesson about being late on the job. Right? I felt just trekking that far to begin a new job was going to put me in good favor. How little I knew.

I had made sure I had stayed behind in New York to enjoy my last weekend — which just so happened to coincide with watching Live Aid on TV (I've always loved pop culture live rock music and special events) — with my then girlfriend before hitting the road Monday morning, while listening to Don Imus on WNBC for the last time. My car had recently been broken into — for the hoard of Cabbage Patch Dolls my friend, Steve, was planning to resell, as well as the car radio — so I was forced to improvise for music. Everyone from Supertramp to Bruce Springsteen, Bryan Adams to Madonna was playing on a boombox running on batteries placed strategically on the front passenger seat.

There was also the matter of my cat, Roxy, named after, yes, one of my favorite groups, Roxy Music.

For some reason, I didn't anticipate how uncomfortable she would be in the car — again, I always learned the hard way — and before I even got over the George Washington Bridge, she was meowing like crazy and distracting me to the point where I had better do something or else.

I don't know how, but I found a veterinarian somewhere in suburban New Jersey who was kind enough to prescribe her some sedatives.

Two nights and three days later, I found myself in America's heartland.

No more thoughts, dreams and prospects of becoming wealthy and famous amid the bright lights of the big city. No more skyscrapers. No more parties and all-nighters and Madison Avenue dreams.

What I was in for was a year of lessons learned, a year of heartache and turmoil, a year that, quite frankly, was the most difficult of my career.

LESSON 4

MASTER YOUR CRAFT

LESSON 4, MASTER YOUR CRAFT
BECOME AN EXPERT IN YOUR FIELD. DEVELOP THE SKILLS NECESSARY TO BECOME INDISPENSABLE ON THE JOB. YOUR DEDICATION AND DETERMINATION WILL PAY OFF IN THE LONG RUN.

1985-1986

I'll always remember that long, lonely drive to Des Moines. I was supposed to start my new job at the start of the week on a Monday, but my inexperience, immaturity and naivety led to me being several days late for it. While I regret not realizing the impact that tardiness would likely contribute to the first impression I made on the job there, I can't fault my younger self for being unprepared for making such a big move so early in my career.

I delayed leaving Brooklyn because of my hankering for a girlfriend I had at the time who I was going to be very sad to leave. Coinciding with the heralded, historic broadcast of the Live Aid concert that weekend for me was a bevy of activities, frivolous to necessary, amid a cloud of emotions.

I didn't know whether I was coming or going. Literally.

You remember Live Aid if you were alive at that time. Not that it was the reason I failed to leave Brooklyn for the Heartland on time, but it certainly factored into the reason I was having such a good time that one last weekend in New York, making it easy to drag my feet. Paul Young's performance of "Everytime You Go Away" comes to mind to this day, as it resonated with me then; I was going away and I sure wished I could take more than a little piece of what I loved about my life in the bright lights of the bright city with me.

But I couldn't take a thing but the memories.

The difference between where I was going and what I was leaving behind was monumental. I probably should have reversed course, but I assumed it was too late to change my mind.

I left town on a Monday morning with my cat, Roxy, crying uncontrollably in the back seat and my boombox in the front seat playing what would be referred to as the best classic rock ever nowadays on cassette tape at high volume.

The next chapter of my work life began three days later.

This was yet another huge, well-known company I was working at, by the way. This was the publisher of a handful of popular, traditional lifestyle magazines such as Better Homes and Gardens, Metropolitan Home, Country Home and Successful Farming.

My job wasn't to write articles for the magazines. That would be a journalist's job. My job was to write direct mail letters for the magazines, helping to promote subscription sales near and far.

Like my stint in my first job out of graduate school, I was again like an apprentice to the stars in this role, learning from some of the best in the business at an early stage in my career.

Funny, as much as I had tried to leave New York City in the rear-view mirror, I ironically was shipped back there to take a three-day, comprehensive seminar led by Joan Throckmorton. She was one of the top direct marketing gurus at the time, and someone from whom I could learn more than a thing or two.

Did you know that the postscript (P.S.) of a letter is often read before the letter itself? Or that you should break the pages of a letter in mid-sentence? Did you know that tokens are involvement devices that your audience members are asked to move from one place in a direct mail package to the order form, which helps trigger a favorable response to your offer?

This is the type of minutiae I learned from Joan. Little-known techniques and strategies that were supposed to increase the response rates of your direct mail marketing efforts. I even learned about the Johnson Box, ("invented" by none other than, you guessed it, a real person named Frank Johnson), a small section at the top of your letter that is supposed to contain a very important message.

I wish I had been more successful at this job, but I did have my moments there. In fact, one of the packages I wrote beat the competition and became a new control.

What's a control? In direct marketing, a control is the package, effort, piece or campaign that gets the highest response rate when implemented. You then test against the control until a new package beats it, which then becomes the new control.

To say you created a control is like saying you are the reigning champion till you are upended by the competition.

At Job 4, I teamed up with a small handful of talented designers including Ben, Mike, Cal and Susan, all friendly people who made hard work a pleasure. We brainstormed together, then divided and conquered. While they handled the colors and pictures, I was the wordsmith, writing billing letters and renewal series, cold mail packages, buckslips, bind-in cards and ads like there was no tomorrow. I learned the importance of writing very short paragraphs (you wanted to give the reader some breathing room) and indenting them, too (white space was a good thing). I wrote teaser copy on outside envelopes to convince recipients to look inside. I put together strong guarantees and calls-to-action as well as catchy headlines and lift notes. I underlined important phrases and made sure certain keywords were highlighted in bold. I turned features into benefits. I proofread my work and presented it to management.

There is always an offer in direct marketing, a call for the recipient to reply. That would be included in a direct mail letter not just once, but a multitude of times. That would be prominently placed on every single component, wherever it made sense. An offer and a strong call to action.

Act now. Call this or that toll-free number. Hurry. Respond immediately. Don't wait. Urgent. Important. Please reply today.

One year free. Free trial offer. Free for a limited-time only. Free with purchase. Your free gift.

The word, free, couldn't be used enough.

You, too. The word "you" worked wonders. Good marketing copy is all about your audience members, the people whose attention — and money — you covet. Butter them up. Speak to their interests, desires and attitudes. Win them over with flattery and praise, empathy and understanding, and you just may win their business.

Such was the life of a young, fledgling direct marketing copywriter. I was a salesman on paper, an anonymous pitchman, an ambassador, a ghost writer for editors, publishers and even people who didn't exist.

Yes, in the world of direct mail, at least back in those days, it wasn't unusual for magazines and other direct mail operations to make up the names and the titles of those who signed the letters. These pseudonyms may have sometimes sounded more impressive, like stage names, but were also used to protect employees' privacy and minimize their accountability. Direct mail — often referred to as junk mail, as far more people than not throw it away without even reading it — was made to appear personal, like it was a one-to-one piece of correspondence — e.g., "dear friend" — what we're really talking about is mass marketing, a relatively impersonal business that banked on high response rates and maximum ROI.

It's a numbers game. Volume was key. Targeting was everything.

On January 28, 1986, I remember gathering around a TV (or maybe it was just the radio... that part I can't remember, but I can't forget the horror of the moment) in Cindy's office, watching the Space Shuttle Challenger blast off into space, only to blow up 73 seconds later. The explosion killed all seven crew members on board, including Christa McAuliffe, a school teacher from Framingham, Massachusetts. My tenure here was not very long, unfortunately. After less than a year living and working in America's heartland, my number was up. My job had been eliminated.

I was determined to return to New York, but I couldn't find another job there. My hopes of working for a big company in a big city had already been dashed, but this was a second chance, perhaps a blessing in disguise.

No such luck came my way, as the only gig I could land was back in my hometown of Franklin, Massachusetts, working for a great company, but a small one still the same. I was back to square one in little time at all, wondering what had gone wrong, worrying if my dreams of becoming a successful marketing professional would ever come true.

LESSON 5

BELIEVE IN *YOURSELF*

LESSON 5
BELIEVE IN YOURSELF
BE FLEXIBLE, RESOURCEFUL AND ADAPTABLE. PURSUE YOUR PROFESSIONAL DREAMS, WHEREVER THAT MAY TAKE YOU. WHEN ONE DOOR CLOSES, ANOTHER ONE OPENS. DON'T BE AFRAID TO TAKE A LEAP OF FAITH.

1986-1987

How ironic. I landed about a mile away from the home in which I grew up. No kidding. After dreaming for years of working in a tall building in the big city where the sky was the limit, I wound up back where I came from, in a small, sleepy town where everyone knew my name.

It was a very good job I had found at a very reputable company with a great reputation not just in Franklin, Massachusetts, but throughout the fundraising industry.

I was thankful for a lot of things, but being back living and working in my hometown was not one of them.

I was determined to make the most of it, though.

Like the gig I had in Des Moines, this one had me doing mostly direct mail, only this time around I was going to be raising funds for nonprofit organizations, not selling subscriptions to magazines. Much more rewarding.

So, in less than four years out of graduate school, I had worked in the music, publishing and fundraising industries. This was my fourth consecutive job in a short period of time, setting a pattern and a pace that would continue throughout my career.

I got bored easily. I wasn't necessarily tired of the work I was doing on the job, but I quickly grew restless with repetition, frustrated with any trace of stagnation. I was always reaching for more. I was always looking for variety.

At this company, I had a great deal of responsibility, writing copy to help raise funds for well-established, highly renowned nonprofit organizations. They did everything from feed the hungry to care for those who were battling cancer, as well as prevent cruelty to animals and provide education to children who were blind.

This was another vertical, fundraising, which I could add to my resume. This was another big change on which I was quickly learning to thrive.

This was also my first agency experience, per se, as opposed to the three client-side jobs I had had to begin my career. At an agency, you are usually working on a variety of projects for a multitude of clients, so like a flock of geese flying in formation, there is a great deal of coordination and collaboration required of the team members.

In the creative department, our deliverable was a so-called transmittal, a thick stack of paper that included everything the client needed to know about our proposed direct mail fundraising package for them.

Our traffic team made sure we kept our projects on schedule, despite the many competing, tight deadlines we faced.

Our account services people were the liaisons, the business side of the operations. We, the writers and the designers, were like the cooks in the kitchen, preparing everything from the appetizers to entrees, hoping the result of our efforts would be received as a piece de resistance.

Together, our words and pictures combined to convince donors and prospects to generously give money to a myriad of well-worthy charitable causes.

I reported to Louise, probably the nicest boss I have had in my career. Such a sweet person, someone who really cared about her colleagues and treated those around her with only the highest degree of respect. I was fortunate to be working for someone so empathetic at a company that was so tight-knit and family-like, an extremely comfortable professional home.

I was lucky to work with Jimmy, too. He was an account executive, a sharp-dressed, well-mannered gentleman who was as articulate as he was smart. He also had a great sense of humor, so there was nothing — I mean, nothing — not to like about him. He was an all-around great guy from whom I learned a lot about how to conduct oneself with the utmost professionalism.

He and I both liked following the local sports teams, too, especially the Boston Red Sox. Our favorite announcer, the late, great Ken Coleman, had this well-known catchphrase whenever someone on the home team hit a home run.

"It's gone," Coleman would exclaim.

Jimmy and I would work that expression anytime we could into our daily banter. If a colleague was away on a business trip? "He's gone." If you left your favorite Cross pen behind at an offsite meeting? "It's gone." If a vendor or supplier happened to drop the ball on an important job? Yup, unfortunately, "They're gone."

The owner of our company, John, was nationally renowned in the fundraising industry, an iconic mastermind, a legendary leader. I hoped someday I could be running the show like him, a man of great integrity and honorable character to the highest degree.

He was an encyclopedia of knowledge when it came to our specialized services. Clients trusted him. Employees listened to him. He was a pillar of the business in which we all earned our livelihood, a gentleman, scholar and guru. Whatever he had to say was tantamount to the gospel on how to succeed in business through hard work, dedication, honesty, collaboration and command of the situation, no matter how challenging.

You could count on John to lead his team in the right direction, carrying every single one of us on his back if at all necessary.

What I liked best about the work I was doing here was that I felt like I was making a difference, not just making a buck. The copy I was writing was helping those who were less fortunate, or at least rallying support for some worthy cause. I could incorporate emotion into the direct mail letters I wrote and tell true stories about good causes and important issues.

I also liked playing racquetball with Tom, one of the top executives at the company. Every so often we'd meet after work to play a handful of games of this fierce, competitive sport that I enjoyed immensely. It wasn't just a workout, it was a ritual that drew us closer, an activity we could share, a time for us to bond and get to know one another in a way that would have been impossible back at the office.

No wonder Tom was so disappointed with me when I eventually told him I was leaving the firm for another job. He was like a mentor to me, someone who trusted me to be committed and loyal. By not confiding in him about my plans beforehand and giving him a chance to make a counter-offer, I'm sure I had let a good friend, my playing partner and professional role model down. My bad.

But I had to do what I thought was right for me at the time. So, after working there at Job 5 for only about a year and a half, I left this small, intimate work environment — not knowing, of course, that I would be returning as a boomerang employee some 13 or so years later — for a company similar in size, but one whose location in the hustling, bustling MetroWest section of the state I liked a lot better.

I was still going to be writing copy, but instead of nonprofit organizations, my clients were going to be magazines. I was going to be working for another agency, but this time around an agency that specialized in circulation promotion.

LESSON 6

PRACTICE **MAKES** *PERFECT*

LESSON 6, PRACTICE MAKES PERFECT
IF AT FIRST YOU DON'T SUCCEED, TRY, TRY AGAIN. BECAUSE EVENTUALLY YOU WILL SUCCEED OVER AND OVER AGAIN. SHARPEN YOUR SKILLS. SPECIALIZE IN SOMETHING. PUT IN THE TIME AND EFFORT REQUIRED TO BE AN EXPERT IN YOUR FIELD.

1988-1990

I was happy to have a window in my new office. I remember looking out of it on my very first day on the job — Monday, January 18, 1988, Martin Luther King, Jr. Day — and seeing fellow employees walking to their cars for a lunch break.

I had plenty of work on my plate already, though. I would be having a bite to eat at my desk, a habit I still have that I established early on in my career, working through that hour of the day in hopes of getting ahead.

Paying my dues is something I've always believed would pay off eventually.

Here I had the opportunity to write for some big-name clients in the publishing industry. Magazines like Consumer Reports, Coin World, Hemmings Motor News, Billboard, Financial Times, Toronto Life, New Age Journal, Spin, Old House Journal and Yankee.

Can you believe it? I couldn't. It wasn't the city, it was Natick, Massachusetts. It wasn't Madison Avenue, it was Speen Street. But it was getting closer to what I expected to be doing at this time in my career.

This was writing day in and day out, from the moment I arrived at the office until everybody else had gone home. I was burning the midnight oil, working like a dog to make sure I was a success on the job. This was going to be a springboard, a launchpad, a pivotal rung on that climb up the corporate ladder with which I seemed to be so obsessed. Not that there weren't going to be at least a few obstacles in my way.

I reported to Tim, a super nice guy and one of the two partners of the agency. Tim was a great manager and a great guy, someone who cared about his employees to the point where you wanted to give him your very best work because of the close bond you had with him, not just for the paycheck.

He and I would take walks every once in a while during lunchtime. I got to know him personally that way, as a friend, not just as a boss. He had an excellent sense of humor, and would often joke around with me like my big brother had done when I was a kid, leading to a relationship with him that I have never quite had with any other supervisor.

His partner, Walter, was looked up to for his knowledge and expertise, and he was known as an industry guru. He was a thought leader, a lead magnet for new client and company growth. I was always impressed by how he carried himself in meetings. When he spoke, employees and clients listened carefully. Walter's words carried a great deal of weight.

I always liked looking out the window of my offices, whether I was working in New York City, Des Moines, or in this case, Natick. I wouldn't call it daydreaming. I would call it coming up for air and a sudden, fresh reminder that there was an outside world beyond the four walls in which I was spending the bulk of my time.

Whenever Walter would leave for an appointment, he would invariably be carrying a big, black portfolio. Inside it was all of the work we had written and designed for all sorts of publications. It would be used as bait to reel in new clients for whom we would eventually reel in new subscribers.

I would be lying if I said I wasn't daydreaming when I looked out the window. I would often picture myself doing that one day, selling my wares like a travelling salesman when I had my own business someday. Just like Walter.

I hardly remember using a computer at my previous job — at my first two jobs, believe it or not, I used an electric typewriter — but I remember exactly what I used to get the job done at this agency, Job 6. I was the proud owner of a brand-spanking-new Macintosh SE, which I bought on credit and was reimbursed for over time by my employer.

I was rocking and rolling now. I was writing more in this job than maybe in my first three marketing jobs combined, accumulating lots of great samples of my work which I could use to establish my own personal portfolio. Like Walter's.

I was also winning awards.

Well, we were winning awards, but I could lay claim to my fair share of at least a few of them from the New England Direct Marketing Association as the copywriter on those honored projects. These were the first awards I had ever won for my work as a copywriter. It was just like the Emmys, Oscars or the Grammys. Okay, maybe not, but it was our industry's version of those famous award shows, and it felt good to be publicly recognized in such a way.

"You like me, you really like me," I couldn't help but say to myself, thinking of Sally Field's famous acceptance speech at the Academy Awards in 1985.

This stage of my career felt like the big time to me even more so than my first two jobs in New York City. My ego was getting stroked. A lightbulb was being lit in my mind. I got this now.

I was getting so comfortable in my role as a burgeoning creative professional, I began to collect toys in my office, like a rubber Gumby, a Bart Simpson doll and a Pee-Wee Herman doll that talked if you pulled the string and said things like, "I know you are, but what am I?"

That was the creative side of me, by the way, the cool agency guy, the copywriter working for a small agency in the suburbs who wanted to feel as though he worked on Newbury Street or Madison Avenue.

"Are we getting our bonus checks today?"

That was me in our staff meetings annoyingly asking Tim about our productivity awards. Management used this formula to determine which of us had produced the most billable work during a certain window of time. I took pride in being prolific and being the winner of those awards at least a few times during my tenure at that job.

On the way into work, I would listen to motivational tapes by speakers like Tony Robbins, Zig Ziglar, Tom Hopkins and Wayne Dyer. I was coming into my own now, realizing I might have what it takes to build my own personal brand. What I lacked in self-confidence, I made up for in determination.

I had written enough letters signed by publishers, editors, circulation directors and billing department executives to feel I knew my craft.

I studied masters like Bill Jayme, Richard Riccelli, Claude Hopkins, David Ogilvy, John Caples and yes, the aforementioned Joan Throckmorton.

I kept a personal swipe file, a big cardboard box filled with mail I received at home that if I examined closely enough, I might find some ideas I could borrow, not steal, and adopt as my own.

I kept the mail we received at home like others collect coins. I read it. I studied it. I did everything I could do to do better than it.

Working with Tim, Walter and my colleagues was always a pleasure. One of the account executives, the people who work closely with the clients, was from my hometown of Franklin. She was super smart. Courtney wouldn't know it, but I learned from her to put the work I wanted to bring home on the floor in front of the door to my office so I wouldn't forget it. I might stumble upon it, but I wouldn't not notice it before I called it a day.

Out of all the art directors I have worked with over the years, I was especially close to Luke. In fact, I still follow his professional journey to this day. He made anything I wrote look spectacular on paper.

Between Tim, Walter, Courtney and Luke, I had a great team of role models and mentors to look up to and emulate. I learned so much from those folks.

The work was too monotonous for me, though, a grind the likes of which I hadn't anticipated. I was putting in more hours than ever, often working on the weekend to keep up with all the deadlines. Eventually I had had enough. I felt I had come so far during my tenure there that I was capable of going it alone. I made plans to say goodbye to the corporate world and hello to life as an entrepreneur.

LESSON 7

REACH
FOR THE
BRASS
RING

LESSON 7, REACH FOR THE BRASS RING
IF YOU CAN DREAM IT, YOU CAN DO IT. DON'T SETTLE FOR LESS. SEIZE THE DAY. GO ABOVE AND BEYOND TO SEPARATE YOURSELF FROM THE COMPETITION. TAKE ADVANTAGE OF THE GIG ECONOMY AND BE YOUR OWN BOSS.

1990-1997

This was the best of times and the worst of times in my career so far. This was when I hung out my own shingle for the first time as a copywriter.

The feeling of freedom was exhilarating, but the threat of bankruptcy was real. Seriously, I was taking a huge leap of faith, not just betting on my talent and capabilities but on my network of friends in the industry as well.

I guess my mother was right when she said back in the day that I always learned by bumping my head. Some things never change.

I was lucky to get some work right away from a former colleague and good friend. To this day, I am grateful to her for her confidence in me. If working in New York City had felt like the be-all and end-all, working on my own was a very close second. "I can get used to this," I said to myself.

Not that I didn't work my tail off. I worked nights, weekends and holidays even more hours than I did at my previous job. I was my own toughest boss. Ever. There were no days off for this chief cook and bottle washer.

The good news was that I could do what I did on my own terms. I didn't have anyone looking over my shoulder, nitpicking my writing, questioning my strategies and critiquing my concepts.

I was the last word, the gatekeeper, the judge and the jury. I was the one who received the kudos and the props from the clients, not any agency suits and executives who had nothing to do with the work itself. It affirmed why I went into this business in the first place. I liked to create. I was happy to have all that authority — and all the responsiblity, too. I didn't mind having to sell my own work. I enjoyed being on the front lines.

One of my earliest promotions was a simple one-page flyer that I had run off at Kinko's, a printing and copying shop down the street, on bright colored sheets of paper. "Take Me To Your Leader," read the headline, asking recipients to introduce me to their managers and supervisors, the people at their office who had the authority to hire freelancers like me. In return for their leads, I provided a little incentive; I would give them a brand-new, crisp one-dollar bill as a reward.

I put these on the doormats of every apartment in the complex where I lived. Out of the hundreds who received them, only a few got back to me. I know, maybe

44

I should have offered a bigger reward than just a dollar, but I had taken the first step as a self-promoter, a giant leap for me as an entrepreneur.

This was what was called guerilla marketing, doing something different than the competition that was aggressive, innovative and unusual. This was something I eventually did regularly, not just for myself, but for my clients in the future.

Although I eventually had an office, I first set up shop in an apartment I shared with my roommate, Larry. Operating on a shoestring budget, I struggled to pay the bills. Suddenly I was paying for my own health insurance — a big financial hit — along with my car payments, rent, utilities, food and so forth. The bills were mounting quickly, while my income was dipping precipitously.

For some reason, Larry and I ended up once at a McDonald's for lunch, only I was flat out of money and afraid my credit card would have insufficient funds if I tried using it. So, there I sat, eating next to nothing (I honestly can't remember if I had anything at all, maybe a small order of fries) while my roommate was chowing down, having no idea, understandably, that I couldn't afford to put food on my plate.

That is what I remember as one of the lowest points on my own in business. It seemed like an interminably long period of time when I couldn't see the forest from the trees, when I wondered whether I was doing the right thing, worried about my future, and fearing for my career.

What comes down must go up, however. I eventually built up steam, taking on a handful of clients at the same time, being able to afford my own office and even put away a decent amount of savings.

This wasn't just any office, either. This was an office in Boston's historic, iconic Faneuil Hall Marketplace, a tourist trap if ever there was one and a reputable, ridiculously awesome address for yours truly. I was so busy, I even hired another copywriter, a move that allowed me to spend less time with my head down in the weeds and more time attending meetings and events, promoting the business and bringing in more clients.

Not that it was all work and no play for me during this time in my career. After closing the office for the day, I would either go out on my mountain bike for a little ride or simply run along the Charles River. I'd even occasionally step into one of the seemingly countless watering holes that dotted both sides of the marketplace.

This ambitious young lad was thriving, both professionally and personally.

Did I tell you I had joined the New England Direct Marketing Association? Remember those awards I had won from New England Direct Marketing Association at my previous job? Well, I became a member of that group shortly after I started my own business in 1990. This was another huge step for me. It was New England Direct Marketing Association that made it possible for me to make so many contacts and meet so many new colleagues in the industry who I could become partners, clients, vendors and miscellaneous resources for me, never mind just plain good friends.

Then there was Toastmasters, a public speaking organization I joined around the same time, that also changed my life.

I, like many others, had a fear of speaking in front of a group of people. While I had taken a public speaking course in college, I gave very few presentations as a professional. In fact, I avoided them.

However, in Toastmasters, I quickly learned how much I loved the thrill and adrenaline of talking in front of an audience, of standing up and speaking my mind from the heart, of being looked at as the expert and entertainer, the leader of the pack.

In Toastmasters, we took turns speaking in front of the others and being critiqued by them. We learned what our strengths and weaknesses were, and over time gained the confidence necessary to speak under any circumstances, even on short notice.

Toastmasters was good to me. I was elected president of our club, a group of about 25 or so of us who met once every couple of weeks. I even won a few speech contests. The experience was a boost to my confidence and a reminder that I was more than just a copywriter in the marketing industry. I was also a communications junkie, and someone who loved to connect with others in any way possible.

Shortly after I joined Toastmasters, I began taking advantage of every opportunity I could in both my personal and professional lives to speak in front of an audience. I gave seminars and taught classes. I spoke at conferences, clubs, colleges and churches. I even got a gig speaking at the Folio conference, traveling annually over the course of a few years to New York City, Chicago and LA to talk about direct mail, marketing and circulation promotion.

I remember using an overhead projector early on in my speaking career, but I eventually had one of those fancy slide projectors with the carousel and remote, toggling through my presentations while talking up a storm about what's what and who's who in my industry.

Speaking in front of a group became part of what I did for a living and something I hope to continue doing for the rest of my life.

Thanks to Toastmasters, I went from a shrinking violet to a force to be reckoned with — if I do say so myself — when it comes to public speaking. I will always be grateful for my experience with this ridiculously awesome organization.

This was the infancy stage of my own personal brand, before anybody even talked about such a thing — that is, the notion of actually being your own brand. I was beginning to carve out a reputation as an influencer and a thought leader. Yay, me.

Woe was me, too, though. With all this authority came a boatload of responsibility, and there were moments when I realized I could be cracking at the seams.

There was no dress rehearsal for what I was doing now on my own. I had no advisors, no mentors and no investors. Nobody whatsoever to guide and support me. It was me against the world.

This was a living. This was my bread and butter. This was the bane of my existence.

I got upset once at Mary, my one and only employee at the time, for taking a long lunch. She was ridiculously talented and incredibly professional in everything she did on the job. I expressed my disappointment. She let me have it right back, and rightfully so. Lesson learned. Chill. As a manager, your job is to hire the right people and give them all the autonomy they deserve. She was the right "people" and then some. She was a superstar, and to this day I regret my overreaction.

Don't be conspicuous in your absence at a big client meeting, either. That's another thing I learned during this time in my career. Especially if you have your name on the door. My sole employee at this time attended an important client meeting on my company's behalf. She represented us exceptionally well, of course, but that still wasn't good enough. The client had invited me to be there, and instead my employee found herself in an impossible situation. It was my bad. There was no excuse for my not being there except for the fact that I had clearly underestimated the importance of face time with the client when you are the principal.

Checking in with your clients at every milestone in the process of doing business with them is a best practice. Don't ever assume anything. I thought it didn't matter if I missed that meeting, but I was forced to think again and again for the rest of my career about that oversight. It was a lesson learned for the ages, as my relationship with that client was never the same.

Face time is never a time to let your guard down in any way, shape or form.

I was gradually losing control of the finances, too. As much as I was bringing in money, I was also reinvesting it in the business and spending an inordinate amount of time chasing down late payments. To say my income was unpredictable would be an understatement. It got so bad, I was paying my employee's wages with a credit card, racking up thousands in debt with next to no promised income.

I've said it before and I'll say it again. I was walking on a high wire without a safety net below.

The autonomy was too good to give up, though. I was doing the best work of my career by far.

Remember those awards I received for my work at my previous job? Well, I won a lot more during this stage of my career, including a Best of Show at the New England Direct Marketing Association Shoestring Awards show for creative excellence in 1993.

Can you believe it? A Best of Show award for sending 50 half-pound bags of coffee to a highly targeted list of potential clients, telling them to wake up and smell the creative, Cargill Creative.

"I can't spill the beans, but I can tell you you'll be receiving a special free gift in the mail soon," said a postcard I had written to them previewing this special free offer.

"Give me the opportunity to perk up your results," I asked my prospects, not knowing at the time that this campaign would not only result in new business, but what would eventually be one of the biggest honors of my career.

I have always taken pride in my ability to think outside of the box, to do things differently than my colleagues and competitors, to stand out in some way from others.

My mailbox campaign was another good example. To illustrate what I did for a living and the professional services I offered my constituency, I bought dozens of metal mailboxes at The Home Depot and had each one of them painted differently by an artist. I then, yes, mailed these mailboxes stuffed with samples of my work to prospective customers, people who I knew were in position to hire me as a freelance copywriter and small creative services agency.

This got me noticed. This got me publicity. This helped get me a reputation as someone who thought differently and uniquely.

For years afterwards, I would occasionally be recognized in business circles as the guy who sent out big, metal, colorfully painted mailboxes to get attention.

I made a name for myself in the direct marketing industry, even if I was just a little fish in a big pond. After receiving those top honors for that campaign, someone, who soon became a very good client, kindly sent me a note, writing something like, "Based on how good you are at promoting your own business, I can only imagine how good you are at promoting your clients." Thanks, Theordore. You were always such a gentleman. And a great client to boot.

Then there was my 151-point checklist. Can you believe it? I came up with 151 different ways — not 10, not 25, but 151 — to assess the merits of a prospective client's direct mail program.

Where do you think I got that idea? Jiffy Lube. Getting my oil changed there one day, the marketer in me couldn't help but be impressed by the checklist they used to mark off what they did to take care of my vehicle. They didn't just check the oil. They looked over my set of wheels from top to bottom.

"I can do that with my own customers," I said to myself. I offered prospects a free audit of their direct mail. I even sent them a prepaid FedEx slip to use when sending me their samples of their work.

Giving so much of my time away was a way for me to show off my expertise and point out areas where I believed I could make improvements to their work if they give me their business in return.

During the best years of Cargill Creative, I would say approximately half of my business was design. I was bringing in the work, handling the copywriting, creative direction, project management and client service. I had the words. The pictures, however, I was outsourcing to a small handful of designers with one of them, Ken, receiving the lion's share of the work.

Ken was an extremely good designer and a great guy as well. He was as easy to work with as he was brilliant at his craft. I was lucky to have him on my team.

Ironically, he was one of the first people I had noticed at one of my first New England Direct Marketing Association meetings. He was surrounded by people there, smiling and shaking hands. He looked like the most popular professional in the room. Assuming he was important, I wanted to get to know him and find out what he did for a living.

Who knew it would only be a matter of time before he would become my go-to designer? He and I were quite the creative duo for a few years, cranking out direct mail packages, ads and brochures for clients of all kinds. I couldn't have asked for a better partner than Ken.

While the bulk of my business was in the publishing and nonprofit fields, I found myself working for a diverse array of clients. I didn't have to travel much. Local clients involved meetings. For others, conference calls usually sufficed. I didn't turn down requests to meet on-site, though.

One such visit necessitated a trip to Long Island, New York. My freelance designer, Liz, and I drove to New London, Connecticut, took the ferry across the sound to Orient Point, where we were picked up for a meeting with Van Bourgondien Tulips. Our job was to create a full-page, four-color ad they could run in a magazine. A typical client kickoff meeting, we received our marching orders and made our way home, only to deliver a week or two later the fruits — or, in this case, the flowers — of our labor. "Color your world beautiful with Van Bourgondien Tulips" was my final approved headline in an ad that I would showcase proudly in my portfolio for years to come.

When my business eventually came to a halt, I felt bad that I wouldn't be able to hand off all that design work to Ken anymore. We had an ideal, mutually-beneficial working relationship. I was going to miss having him by my side. And Liz and other designers, freelancers, contractors and clients, too.

I enjoyed the run on my own, though. These years of my career helped establish myself not just another copywriter, but a thought leader, a public speaker, a businessman and an entrepreneur. I learned that when your name is on the business, your reputation is everything. You can't hide behind anyone or anything. You're fully exposed, weaknesses and all.

The potential pitfalls are not to be taken lightly. The risks are considerable, but the rewards are unparalleled.

I was called "Framingham's Junk Mail King" in an article in the Metrowest Daily News, featuring a big color picture of me in my office behind a stack of, well, junk mail.

The awards began to come along with the invitations to speak, too. My peers in the industry gave me more trust and respect. I was on the front lines. I had people's ears and I was able to hold their attention. I was lucky to have their business. It was a wild and bumpy ride.

Like I said earlier, it was the best of times and the worst of times. Along with all the good things that were suddenly happening to me came a ton of things that were next to impossible to either keep up with or simply overcome, either emotionally or financially.

I went into debt. I had to let go of an employee — sadly. I worked on weekends. I paid for my own insurance. I chased down late payments. I hired freelancers and interns. I wrote up contracts and proposals, not just direct mail and ads. I made phone calls and sent faxes. I drove to FedEx to make deliveries. And I cried — no, sobbed uncontrollably — one night when I lost a prestigious piece of new business.

Seriously. I had written the direct mail package of my life for a large, well-known publication. Or so I thought. I worked my tail off on that project. It included a long direct mail letter and several other components, each of which had been carefully worded by yours truly. I had worked on dozens of projects like this one before, but never one with such great potential. I nailed it. Or so I thought. I pulled out all the stops in my work for this client, going above and beyond to ensure success.

Only that wasn't enough. I had fallen short for some reason. The project was killed, something I have witnessed less than a small handful of times in my entire career. My feelings were crushed. My tears were unstoppable.

Being your own boss isn't as easy as it seems. The freedom is unbeatable. The tradeoff, though, can be painful. I have always been an independent spirit, someone who thrives on autonomy, doing my very best work when no one is looking over my shoulder and contributing their two cents.

But this business is subjective, writing copy and being innovative, recommending strategies, concepts, tactics and tips.

And it is a serious business, not an exercise in creativity. Everything we do is measured. ROI rules.

The best job I ever had was coming to an end. It was time for another change. What was old was going to be new again. What I had thought might be permanently in the rear-view mirror was now smack dab in my face.

But not before one last hurrah, and one final, futile attempt to breathe new life into this little dream of mine.

Out of the blue came an offer to buy what was left of Cargill Creative, an offer too good to refuse. A fellow direct marketing professional, Joshua, was interested in absorbing my business. He had a small agency of his own. In exchange for my clients and expertise, he would provide me with an office and a job, positioning what I had to offer as an extension of his company's services.

I moved out of my Speen Street, Natick location and set up shop in a big, newly renovated office in Needham, where I had a small team of colleagues to collaborate with, including a sales team and a designer.

Despite the amazing accommodations and warm hospitality, though, for some reason I was uncomfortable having to share anything to do whatsoever of what I had built on my own. Something was wrong with me. It wasn't them. Something was bothering me about this seemingly ideal partnership.

While I couldn't identify the problem, I certainly knew the solution. I couldn't let go partly, so I had to let go completely of a balloon that had already burst.

"Can we take a walk outside?" I asked Joshua, my new partner, one day only a few months into our new venture. I laid it on the line. I had to move on. I had to reestablish myself as a full-time employee elsewhere and shed all ties to my own business for the time being. I needed a new beginning, not a continuation of something that hadn't been working in the first place.

For some strange reason, certainly unforeseen, in a classic case of careful what you wish for, I was now tired of what I had seemingly wanted all along. The glory wasn't as great as the burden of being an entrepreneur was heavy.

I needed a big change.

LESSON 8

BE CAREFUL
WHAT
YOU
WISH FOR

CHAPTER 8
BE CAREFUL WHAT YOU WISH FOR

YOUR PROFESSIONAL LIFE IS A SERIES OF TRADEOFFS. YOU CAN'T HAVE THE GOOD WITHOUT THE BAD. ALWAYS LOOK ON THE BRIGHT SIDE OF YOUR ROLE AND RESPONSIBILITIES, BUT BE PREPARED TO MAKE SOME SACRIFICES. MAKE THE MOST OF EVERY OPPORTUNITY THAT COMES YOUR WAY.

1997-1999

Like many of the jobs I got during the earlier stage of my career, this one wasn't particularly hard to get. I had a phone call, an interview and then a new job. Boom.

The trade-off was going from being the big cheese, only having to answer to only my own clients, to feeling like just another cog in the wheel, a small fraction of how important I felt at the helm of my own ship.

Not that this company in Woburn, Massachusetts, wasn't an outstanding organization. It was a blue-chip agency with a stellar reputation.

After having grown accustomed to being my own boss and having my own space, though, I was now just one of a couple hundred or so employees. I was given no choice but to sit in a cubicle, the first cube of my career.

I know, I was spoiled. I had created a monster that I would have to live with forever, that monster being the experience of having been my own boss. After having that taste of professional independence, autonomy and freedom, there was no going back to the corporate world as a fully satisfied employee. That monster in my mind would always be reminding me of good days gone by. I wasn't just spoiled, I was destined to always feel like my career had been at least partly a failure.

The good news was that the work at this agency was as fantastic as was the treatment I received from my colleagues. My counterparts in the creative department were incredibly skilled and quite laid-back. Not only did I learn from them, I had fun with them, joking around, listening to music and talking shop.

I also worked with some outstanding account executives, people who were amazingly accomplished at project management, client service and taking responsibility for the business side of things. Unlike those of us who were paid for being creative, they were tasked with being buttoned up and detail-oriented, focused on sales and success rather than the actual development of the work.

They were the liaisons between the agency and its customers, the gatekeepers of the deliverables. They approved our copy and design before the clients ever saw it. If they liked what we did, chances were high that the clients would like it, too.

One of my co-workers was responsible for the trafficking and triaging of all the projects we had in the queue. She would come around with a list of my priorities for the day. Her job was to make sure we were working on the right project at the right time. I couldn't have felt more supported.

And our creative director, Christopher, was one of the best bosses I've had in my career. A gifted writer, he was unassuming and understated in his approach as a creative director, a true gentleman who trusted his team members with the autonomy they required to put their own imprimatur on their work.

I didn't realize how good I had it in having Christopher as my superior.

He actually listened to me. I had given him a list of recommendations at one point, my honest opinion on where I thought we might be able to level up. He wasn't just open to hearing me out. He acted on many of my suggestions.

Good for you, Christopher. And thank you so very, very much. To this day, I think of you as one of the nicest guys I have met in this business.

At this agency, my clients were in the publishing, insurance, high-tech and financial sectors. Fairly big brands. My portfolio became much more diversified here. From the corporate culture to the people to the work itself, this was as much like working in a Madison Avenue-like advertising agency as I had experienced to date.

My words jumped off the paper they were printed on thanks to some of the most talented designers I have worked with in my career. Sam. Gordon. Scarlett. Will. Thank you for being such good working partners.

From direct mail packages to postcards, self-mailers to brochures, I wrote headlines and body copy for a multitude of formats and an array of different clients.

I felt good about my professional self during this time in my career, especially when the company featured me as an offer in a trade show giveaway. After a quick, albeit flattering photo shoot, my picture was displayed on a promotional piece that announced recipients could be treated to a free presentation by yours truly if they were the lucky winners in our contest.

Despite the letdown of having to let go of my own business, I had never felt so prized — as an employee — in my life. What did I do to deserve such recognition? How would I live up to expectations? What do I do for an encore? These were just some of the many questions running through my anxious head at that time.

I was at once confident and worried, optimistic and hesitant. I had the professional world in the palm of my hand, but I couldn't hold onto it for long, as you'll soon see.

Not only was I succeeding as an associate creative director at this agency, I was also becoming more involved as a board member of the New England Direct

Marketing Association, which you'll remember I had joined years ago when I had started my own business. I was working my way up the corporate ladder, one rung at a time, establishing myself as an award-winning creative guy, public speaker and thought leader.

I even resurrected my involvement in Toastmasters, starting our own club there at this company, serving as its president for almost a year until I left for my next gig.

This was one of those rare opportunities to shine in a way my colleagues would not have seen otherwise. This was an extracurricular event, something outside of the daily grind that excited everyone who participated. About 20 of us would gather every couple of weeks or so to give presentations in front of one another. You saw a side of others in the office you never could have imagined. Someone who was quiet and heads-down might suddenly surface as a dynamic leader, given the support and encouragement of our group. They might take that newfound confidence and use it to achieve greater success on the job, too. Such was the benefit of taking part in Toastmasters, something I was grateful to know that my employer understood.

During that time, I'd say I was once again feeling my oats, to put it mildly. I was enjoying my status as an emerging industry luminary — at least that's how it felt to be me at that juncture. I was caught between the independent, scrappy writer I was by trade and a life as a successful business executive that could be mine if I could only stay the course.

I was easily distracted and distressed, though, by my surroundings in the office. I was accustomed to solitude and privacy while I worked, not the chatter and interruptions that came with the corporate territory. I was impatient and inconsolable, unwilling, if not unable to accept this dramatic change in my work life. It was my first taste of what a real job would look like for me after having owned my own business, the beginning of a cycle of disruptive sudden, job changes that wouldn't end for a couple decades.

During lunch, I'd drive to this small, nondescript parking lot in the neighboring town of Wakefield next to Lake Quannapowitt, where I'd eat my bag lunch and take a good, albeit quick power nap. Somehow, I'd wake up without an alarm clock and make it back to work on time. No harm, no foul. If anything, I would be more refreshed and invigorated for the second half of the day.

A few times, I was treated to lunch by the owner of the company, which was an extremely flattering and kind gesture on his part. As much as I was happy and honored to be having a bite to eat with him, I don't think I realized at the time how much confidence that meant he had in me. I underestimated my worth when I should have been capitalizing on it.

I'm not going to lie, though. I have always questioned my abilities and undermined my chances for even greater success at some of the most pivotal times in my career for reasons unbeknownst to me.

Since I was knee-high to a grasshopper, I have struggled with low self-esteem. I have never felt good enough. So, at times like these, ironically, I would either think the success I was enjoying wasn't deserved — that it was being inappropriately given to me, not earned — or that it paled in comparison to what I should be accomplishing at this juncture in my life, especially compared to my peers, colleagues, friends and family members. I vacillated between imposter syndrome and delusions of grandeur.

Either way, this confusion and second-guessing of my own worth has invariably led me to move on to the next challenge as quickly as I feel I have overcome the existing one.

So yes, unsurprisingly to me, I got itchy at this agency in short order. Because of my involvement in the New England Direct Marketing Association and the industry at large, I heard about plenty of opportunities that maybe could be mine if I decided to go in a different direction. So it was only a matter of time before I scratched that itch.

I started looking around after only about a year there, having conversations with potential new employers and jumping on the phone during those lunchtime getaways.

It was at a New England Direct Marketing Association meeting where I heard about the next stop on my career journey. Someone was looking for someone like me. This appeared to be a perfect new job opportunity. Closer to home. Small team of creative people. Doing what I do best. It was a chance to be doing some creative directing, copywriting and even contributing to the leadership of this agency.

What could go wrong?

LESSON 9

PATIENCE
IS A
VIRTUE

LESSON 9, PATIENCE IS A VIRTUE

THE GRASS ISN'T ALWAYS GREENER ON THE OTHER SIDE OF THE FENCE. SO, DON'T BE SO AMBITIOUS THAT YOU JUMP AT THE FIRST OPPORTUNITY TO MOVE. DON'T TAKE ANYTHING FOR GRANTED. SOMETIMES WHAT YOU'RE SEARCHING FOR IS RIGHT IN FRONT OF YOU.

1999

This could have been the last stop on my career journey as opposed to just a pit stop. Everything seemed to be perfectly in place.

Even though I was treated with the utmost respect from my colleagues at my last job, especially upper management, I hungered for more authority, to be a bigger fish in a smaller pond, and this was my chance.

I was brought in at the VP level at this job in Newton, Massachusetts, charged with helping to manage the staff and grow the company. I would also do some copywriting, which was my bread and butter, of course.

This was a relatively small creative shop, led by June, a very strong and talented leader.

I'll never forget one of my first client meetings with June. It was at a large, renowned, well-established company in the Boston area run by a family who had owned the place for years. The top dog was a brilliant, prominent businessman and public figure.

While sitting only a couple feet away from me, he looked me straight in the eye and asked why they should do business with us.

Now was not the time to hem, haw and stammer, although I was certainly feeling the heat. After all, I was new on the job and had never been placed in this position.

We ended up, in fact, doing business with that company despite my less than stellar performance in answering that question, and I ended up learning a big lesson in business. Always have your elevator pitch in your back pocket. Never be caught off guard. You want to commit to memory your key talking points and anticipate any objections your prospect may have to what you have to offer.

You don't get a second chance to make a first impression.

I've gone on a lot of company outings over the years, but I never had an experience like the one I had working for this company.

The 15 or so of us who worked there were entered in a canoe race along the Charles River in Dedham. I was paired with Rick, an art director at the company. The adrenaline was flowing. Perhaps too much, though. As soon as we started, we flip-flopped and capsized into the water, probably because we were both so aggressive in paddling, and not paying attention to how our weight might be shifting uncontrollably. While we were probably underwater for only a few seconds, it seemed like an eternity. We both resurfaced safely, thankfully, but I'll never forget the legit momentary fear I felt.

A couple people I had worked with at my previous job in Woburn joined me in taking new positions at this agency. Ron was a very talented designer. Meanwhile, Jim was relatively new to the industry, but a prodigiously smart marketing professional whose focus at the time was writing. Two great guys.

One of the many projects I worked on at this agency was a radio campaign for a large private university in Boston. An assignment like this didn't come around often, so I was particularly enamored with it and anxious about the results.

For some reason, Jim and I were tag-teaming the scripts, writing up different versions of the same pitch for the announcer. Not that I remember the details, but I'll never forget how uncharacteristically angry I got at him when he pushed back on some of my feedback. I don't think I've ever been so mad in my professional life. It was a poor lack of self-control on my part that I regret to this day. All over a silly difference of opinion over a simple choice of words.

Fortunately, it was just a one-sided, short-lived temper tantrum, but I was ashamed of myself — embarrassed and mortified — and sent him a written note of apology afterwards. Sorry, Jim.

Another lesson learned the hard way by me. Never lose your cool. Even if you're in charge. Even if you believe you're right. Never lose your cool on the job. Never lose your cool anywhere. Never. Ever. Period.

While most of the work we did there was print and direct mail, I also worked on those radio scripts and a few online banner ads. This was really around the time my work began to consist of not just traditional media, but digital media, too. Email was a thing now. Everybody needed a website and online advertising was booming.

But this job was apparently never meant to be, unfortunately, even though it may have been the best opportunity of my career. It was a small agency. I was recruited. It was located not too far from home. I was in my element. My feeling is that it was either too good to be true, or the chemical imbalance in me decided that I was not to have it so easy.

Seriously. I have dealt with anxiety, depression and OCD since I was a teenager, and I have overanalyzed practically every good thing that has come my way over the years. I am prone to self-destructive, sabotaging behavior that undermines my own chances for success. Sometimes I can't get out of my own way.

This could have been my dream come true. My name could have been on the door. I admit it. I blew it. I was in the prime of my life in the marketing profession and I had the chance to co-manage an agency, an agency I would never have been able to build on my own, an agency the likes of which would never come into my grasp all the rest of my years working in this industry.

June had faith in me. Her employees believed in me. For some reason, I clearly couldn't handle it.

Like that moment I had fallen into the water in the canoe with Rick on the Charles River, I was in over my head and almost couldn't save myself from drowning.

Toward the end of my tenure there, June was planning to relocate the agency into bigger space. While shopping around for new real estate with her, we looked at an old, historic church one day in Newton that included a ridiculously awesome office ensconced toward the very top of a steeple. For a moment, I was on top of the world, surrounded by a window view of the city below. I could see cars racing up and down the Mass Pike, the Boston skyline, suburban neighborhoods, local businesses and buildings no matter which way I turned. I felt like I could be sitting at a desk here soon, doing my thing, managing a team, and helping to run a business. I knew that wasn't going to happen, though. I knew that it was too good to be true.

It couldn't have been too many days after that brief, bold moment in what could have been my own ivory tower, I found myself embroiled in a tense meeting in June's office, reviewing the status of one of our projects, and debating who among a small team of us sitting at the table was going to get on the phone with the client.

This wasn't an emergency. It was par for the course in the life of an agency professional. This wasn't something to get upset about, but for some reason my patience with the corporate world decided it had run its course for the time being.

I was out the door within minutes, not just the door of the office we were in, but the door of the building. I was in my car and on the road, on my way home for the day before I knew it. I found myself pulling over to the side of the road and meandering through a big, desolate field of tall grass contemplating my professional future, or whatever was going to be left of one. I was setting the stage for my exit from that job and for yet another disappointment in my career. Not anyone's fault but mine.

At our next traffic meeting, I announced my departure after having shared my feelings privately with my boss. I had grown frustrated with my role, feeling I was spending too much time in management and not enough time on the creative product itself.

June had been a great partner. Not only had I been unable to meet my own unrealistic expectations, I didn't have enough control of the situation to feel confident of my future there.

Yup. I was up a creek without a paddle and afraid I would drown.

LESSON 10 KEEP ON KEEPING ON

LESSON 10, KEEP ON KEEPING ON
IT'S NOT HOW OFTEN YOU FALL DOWN, BUT HOW QUICKLY YOU GET BACK ON YOUR FEET. PUT YOUR DISAPPOINTMENTS AND FAILURES IN THE REAR-VIEW MIRROR. LEARN FROM YOUR MISTAKES AND REBOUND YOUR WAY INTO NEW OPPORTUNITIES FOR FULFILLMENT AND SUCCESS.

1999-2000

One thing I've been in both my personal and professional lives is perseverant. I may have fallen down a lot over the years, but I've always gotten back up. This juncture in my career was no different.

Somehow, a former colleague and client of mine, Elizabeth, found out I was looking for a new job, and she happened to have one that appeared to be tailor-made for me.

Serendipity strikes again.

In no time at all, I was back in the saddle, this time around helping to start a small, in-house ad agency for a publishing company based in Watertown, Massachusetts, just a few miles away from the previous stop on my professional journey.

I was grateful for the opportunity and excited to be reunited with Elizabeth, who was wicked smart, super strategic, a pleasure to work with and an outstanding conversationalist.

I was raring to go from day one.

Not only did we hardly have a staff, though, we didn't have an online presence, which was a marketing imperative for every business organization at the turn of the century. I don't recall even having any clients. We were starting from the bottom.

When I say we, I am talking about Brett, who was an existing employee there. He was my partner in crime, so to speak, from the outset. We eventually hired both a designer, Emily, and a traffic manager, Alexander.

There wasn't a dull moment among this fearsome foursome at the office on Walnut Street, but unfortunately, there didn't seem to be much of a future there, either. We brought in a few clients in due time, but sadly, try as we might, it seemed like we were spinning our wheels more than we were going places.

I needed to "bring the kill to the cave," according to Elizabeth, who was now my boss. I understood what she was saying. I knew my shortcomings. I had my weaknesses.

I interpreted her charge as meaning that I needed to be more of a salesman and less of a creative guy, considering the success or failure of this new venture was all but riding on my shoulders (at least that's how I felt). I relished, never mind appreciated, the challenge, but I had a feeling early on that we were fighting an uphill battle that would be difficult to win. Not a good mindset, I realize, when you're leading the charge at the helm. My bad, utterly.

The good news is that we created a very impressive website for ourselves, if I do say myself. It was thoroughly modern and up-to-date, positioning ourselves for bigger things to come, hopefully.

Yes, for a while, it felt like we were hitting our stride and heading in the right direction, even though we weren't lacking distractions and reasons to worry about our future.

For instance, Brett was fond of wearing a baseball hat to work, and I — being old-school, I suppose — didn't think it made the right impression on clients. What do you think? I didn't care if we were located in the middle of nowhere. I wanted us to look like we were running with the big dogs on Madison Avenue.

My argument didn't go very far. After airing our differences of opinion, there was a semblance of a compromise at least.

Brett was right. I was wrong. I had to chill. A familiar refrain for me, if not others, too.

This was the beginning of the end of dress codes in the office — wherever you worked — anyway. A fancy Brooks Brothers suit was a fashion statement of the past. I had to force myself to dress down in order to fit in with the younger set. The upside is that we did some excellent work together during our stint together as an agency. We even worked on a TV ad, the only one I have ever worked on in my career.

Some of our best work was for ourselves, though.

We put together that ridiculously awesome website. We sent out a great series of postcards to promote our business. We created an excellent lead generation campaign that had me writing up recommended marketing plans for potential new clients. We even had hats made with our logos on them. I still have some of those hats down in my cellar, now that I think about it, over 20 years later.

We had it all going on, except for turning a profit. Our days were numbered, and I could see the writing on the wall. Damn. My time had come and gone once again in the blink of any eye.

"You are running away from something, not toward anything," said Elizabeth, or at least something to that effect.

She may have been right. I have always been a little bit paranoid, leery of competition, therefore trying to keep one step ahead of others in order to avoid conflict and failure. I have always struggled with ambivalence and uncertainty.

65

Understandably, she was let down when I announced my departure, but it was already too late. I had made up my mind. I was on my way out the door.

Where I was going next, of course, was another thing. I was crossing my fingers that I was moving onward and upward. Time would certainly tell.

Part of me now still feels shame for making such an impractical decision — and not for the first or last time. There are no excuses. I ought to have known better. You should never leave a job without having something else lined up. On the other hand, I've always believed that you only live once. I've always run like a caged lion set free. I've always said to myself, c'est la vie.

LESSON 11

DON'T BURN BRIDGES

LESSON 11
DON'T BURN BRIDGES
BUILD A FRIENDLY, SUPPORTIVE NETWORK OF INDUSTRY PEERS, PEOPLE WHO HAVE YOUR BACK WHEN THE CHIPS ARE DOWN. LEARN FROM THEM. GROW WITH THEM. THE MORE OFTEN YOU LEND THEM A HAND, THE MORE LIKELY THEY'LL BE TO LEND YOU THEIRS WHEN YOU NEED THEM.

2000

I either had good luck or I was good at what I did for a living. Maybe it was a combination of both. The next job always seemed to fall in my lap.

I couldn't seem to find the right job, though, a home for my career forever, if it even existed.

Of course, that didn't go unnoticed among my peers and colleagues. I remember being called a "short-timer" once after having announced I was leaving a job. Ouch.

That was also a common interview question. "So, it seems you have not stayed in one job for very long, Bob. If you are offered this job, how do we know you'll stay with us for more than a year or two?"

My answer was always that my intentions were to stay at my next job for the rest of my career. I wanted stability. I was a loyal lieutenant. But the truth was seemingly written on the wall. Commitment to one job did not come easy for me, despite my dedication to my craft and my love for the industry in which I earned my livelihood.

"I wish I owned stock in whoever makes your business cards," a fellow direct marketer would often joke whenever he heard I had taken a new job. "I'd be a millionaire."

Another friend in marketing once asked what the over-under, similar to sports betting, was on my tenure at my next place of employment. "Two years? Three years?"

The joke was on me.

Fortunately, it didn't take very long before I heard about an opportunity that appeared to be aligned with my background, skills and expertise. Someone I knew from a former job — deja vu, I know — told me about an open position at a small, boutique-like advertising agency on Newbury Street in Boston.

The pay was in line with what I was earning at this time in my career, the job title was perfect (associate creative director), my boss (to be) was extremely smart, my colleagues (to be) were super nice and the work was right up my alley.

They had me at hello.

At this gig, I wrote a lot of banner ads, emails and other copy for online marketing campaigns, which was great for my portfolio, as the digital era was upon us and it behooved me to have this type of experience.

68

However, I soon became worried about my job security there. We were owned by a dot-com company in Maynard, a small working-class town west of Boston, that sold e-books, a relationship that clouded my vision of our future.

One saving grace for me was the upscale location on Newbury Street, which meant I got to walk through the beautiful Public Garden every day on my way back and forth to the office from the Boston Common underground garage.

I also liked to stroll around Copley Square during lunchtime, often taking in all the sights and sounds of the city from the comfort of a park bench while having a quick bite to eat.

The pace, nor the work itself, wasn't a challenge, but for some reason I felt like I was falling off the rails. It was though I was just along for the ride — a passenger, not the conductor — a long, strange train trip wherever it took me, even if I knew in my heart that that wasn't how I rolled.

The good news was that this was the beginning of my online transformation, when a lot of my writing was being done for the web, not necessarily for print and direct mail. I was heading in the right direction. I was teetering on the cusp of what was soon to be a reality, a focus on digital, not traditional marketing.

However, the fruits of my labor were not enough to offset how unappreciated I felt in this role. Let me be clear. This pessimistic feeling was on me. I was being treated well. There were plenty of opportunities here. I was just struggling once again with my self-esteem and need to stand out. Despite my very best efforts, I felt invisible and overlooked, like a transient without a place to live.

Luck would have it, though, that within only a few months, like a minor leaguer being called up to the big leagues, I was transferred over to this agency's parent company in Maynard, Massachusetts, a stone's throw from where I lived in Sudbury. The 12-minute commute promised to be the shortest of my career, counting the three or four stops signs and one set of lights I was forced to tolerate.

Woe wasn't me.

LESSON 12

EMBRACE
TECHNOLOGY
NOW

LESSON 12, EMBRACE TECHNOLOGY NOW
BE AN EARLY ADOPTER OF WHAT'S NEW AND DIFFERENT IN TECHNOLOGY. DON'T BE A LAGGARD. DEVELOP A DIGITAL-FIRST MINDSET. ANTICIPATE CHANGE AND ADAPT QUICKLY TO WHAT'S COMING DOWN THE PIKE.

2000-2001

Now it felt like I had a home, a professional home. At least it did for a while. And what a spread this was, my first real taste of the digital life. I'm talking all-in, 100% online marketing, as in one of those early dot-com companies you've read about. And while this chapter doesn't necessarily have a happy ending, it wasn't even close to an unendurable stop along my corporate journey.

In fact, this stop was exciting. This stop was enjoyable. For once, work didn't seem like work. Work seemed like a page out of a science fiction novel in which I was one of the leading characters. I was watching the future of business unfold, albeit in vain, before my eyes.

We were ahead of our time. E-books were us. My job was to write copy about these books for various marketing materials, including an electronic newsletter of which I oversaw the production and distribution.

I was on the ground floor of what would eventually be a revolution in communications, but unfortunately, this company's days were numbered.

Not that these weren't super smart professionals. They were some of the most intelligent people I have ever worked with, from those in the C suite down to my colleagues in the cubes. They were also ridiculously easy to work with, to the point that I loved coming into the office every day, a feeling I can't say I've had everywhere else. I was working with incredibly kind human beings, completing wicked cool projects for an ultra-modern company located just down the road from home.

Yet another too-good-to-be-true scenario.

No kidding. Almost as fast as I became comfortable there, rumors began circulating about our potential demise.

I couldn't catch a break.

Layoffs were inevitable. Layoffs came quickly. I was one of the last to be let go along with dozens of others, each of us holding onto the job like a buoy on rough waters.

As we were invited into the conference room to receive the dire news, we looked at each other with blank stares, knowing fully and sadly well what was to come. This was the moment we dreaded. This was the last meeting we would have together.

Like countless other companies around this time, this dot-com was now — sadly — a dot-bomb, written up in the history books as yet another dream business not to come true.

E-books were going to be a thing one day, a big thing, but not so fast. Companies like ours were going to be the norm in the future, but apparently we had rolled the dice just a little too soon.

LESSON 13 CHANGE IS *CONSTANT*

LESSON 13, CHANGE IS CONSTANT

BE PREPARED TO PROVE YOURSELF OVER AND OVER AGAIN. YOU'RE ONLY AS GOOD AS YOUR LAST SUCCESSFUL PROJECT, IF NOT WHAT YOU'RE WORKING ON NOW. PUT YOUR BEST FOOT FORWARD AND HIT THE GROUND RUNNING. ADOPT A DON'T-STOP-WON'T-STOP MENTALITY REGARDLESS OF THE CIRCUMSTANCES.

2001-2004

As quickly as all the years had gone by, what I realized around this time in my career was that each of my job changes was a significant loss, a dream disappointedly dashed and a big blow to my ego, despite the fact that I was moving on each time around to what promised to be a better opportunity and fit for me.

Every job left behind was like something had died. Grieving was inevitable, but how much so depended on how happy I was in my next role.

I was saying goodbye to people I had grown accustomed to working with, friends I had made and work I had done, suddenly exchanging a familiar situation for something entirely new, something I had to learn from scratch.

I was starting all over again time after time, earning credibility, building trust and developing relationships.

Try as I might, I also couldn't shake the feeling that I was to blame for all this churn. Never mind the few times I was let go, or even when there was every good reason that I had tendered my resignation.

Emotionally and realistically thinking, I couldn't help but feel that it was a bad mark against me. After all, unfortunately and often unfairly, frequent job changes have historically been frowned upon.

These fits and starts had certainly taken a toll on me, but I honestly feel they made me a stronger professional and better prepared for whatever came my way, both professionally and personally.

After the mass layoffs at the dot-com, I found myself, well, unemployed.

I didn't have another job lined up and I was receiving unemployment benefits for the first time in my life.

Wait! What?

Here I was aspiring to be some wealthy, highfalutin senior-level executive in Manhattan by this time in my career and instead, I was ensconced in my dingy attic office in the sleepy, little town of Sudbury, alone with my resume, cover letter and a big, fat Rolodex that was on its last legs.

Who knew what opportunities would arise down the road? For now, I was pondering a future without a steady paycheck and a workplace to call my home away from home.

Never being one to procrastinate, in addition to a lot of phone calls, emails, mailings, networking and the like, I launched a novel project that I thought might help me find my next gig. I began writing a daily blog about my search for a new job. I called this blog, "Suddenly Solo."

This could be looked at as one of my earliest experiences with social media, as it met all the criteria for being characterized as such: it was an online journal, it was updated regularly and readers could subscribe to it to ensure they would receive every single one of my daily posts.

The medium was tailor-made for someone like myself, as I loved writing about both my personal and professional lives and sharing it with as many people as possible. Not only was this project cathartic for me, giving me the opportunity to get my feelings about being in between jobs off my chest, but it was also strategic. It kept me in front of potential employers and referrals, fellow marketing professionals who might be able to help me land my next gig.

Besides all the emails, letters, phone calls, interviews and meetings that were a part of this time in my career, "Suddenly Solo" was yet another means of getting the word out about my marketing prowess and availability for immediate hire. I certainly had fun with it, not hesitating to share my feelings about being temporarily — hopefully — unemployed as well as about my entire career up to this point.

The following post is from a daily blog, Suddenly Solo, that was written by Bob Cargill for a month or so during this time...

On May 1, 2001, I was one of 39 employees who lost their jobs when our employer, a dot-com company, regrettably had to cease operations. I began keeping an online journal the very next day. I called it "Suddenly Solo."

At first, I looked at "Suddenly Solo" as a good way to get the word out that I was, well, suddenly solo and looking for a new job. I emailed my friends and colleagues, asking them if I could add them to my list of subscribers. Then, only if they had "opted in," they received each entry of my journal, on the day that it was written, by email. In an attempt to expand my network, I also introduced a "viral" component to this project, asking subscribers to forward it along to their own list of contacts with their endorsement. Finally, I began hosting "Suddenly Solo" here on my Web site, sending a simple alert to subscribers whenever something new was written, asking them to visit my site in order to read the latest entry. From here, they could click through to read the whole story at http://www.bob123.diary-x.com, where it is now archived.

For 58 long and lonely days, "Suddenly Solo" was the vehicle by which I expressed myself to an audience of readers who seemed genuinely interested in what I had to say. Yes, I used my journal to draw out job leads. But it evolved into much more than just a networking tool. It became a labor of love, an account of my emotional state, a test of my fortitude.

Fortunately, on June 28, 2001, I was able to post my last entry, which I called the swan song for a journal that had been the saving grace for me during such an interminable time of my life. I had been offered a new job. I was suddenly solo suddenly no more.

Not surprisingly, despite the broad outreach I had done with my network in the industry, the job I was waiting for came quite easily. The offer came from someone I knew, who was currently working at a place I already worked at once before in my career. Paul, who was going to be leaving his post as Senior Creative Director at this preeminent direct response fundraising agency, recommended me for the job to his superiors there. I had the inside track. And just like that, in a matter of weeks, I had the job.

It was times like these that I realized I was blessed. If that was the longest I would ever be out of work — about 60 days — I should be grateful. Who knew I would find myself employed by the same company twice in my career? Who knew I would become a boomerang employee over 12 years later?

This was deja vu. This was my opportunity to work at the same great place for a second time. This was me being lucky enough to be working at this first-class firm full of ridiculously nice people yet again.

Thanks, Paul. Your recommendation meant so much to me. Thanks, Susan, my new boss, who clearly had enough faith in me to bring me on board at that time.

The job here this time around, though, was a significant change of pace for me. Not only was I managing a large creative team, I was also traveling quite a bit, more so than I had at any other time in my career. As if that wasn't enough, I was writing a ton of direct mail fundraising copy whenever I wasn't needed in meetings.

The demands on me as a professional had just increased exponentially.

As did the status. It felt good to finally be in the role I felt I deserved. This was an executive position, one that made me especially proud to be a marketer. I was happy to be working not just for a buck, but for a variety of great causes and well-known non-profit organizations that were making a big, positive difference in the world.

I relished being a manager of a large team of about 15 creative professionals. We had regular team meetings at which I did my best to motivate the troops. I walked around the office frequently to check in on everybody, one at a time. I carried out my belief in positive reinforcement and carved out a reputation as someone my colleagues could talk to about anything. I was there to support as much as to direct, to listen as much as to tell.

I had the opportunity to speak at many meetings, both internally and on location with clients, and even lead some of these meetings. Being involved with new business pitches was something I particularly enjoyed, especially showing off the work of the creative team.

To win a new client, we often had to develop brand-new creative work (called spec, short for speculative) on our own dime and time, which would hopefully impress the prospect enough that they would want to hire us. This would take shape as examples of what we would do for them if we were to be hired. It was a great deal of work and certainly a risk, but in those days it was the norm. Think of it as a way of auditioning for the job should you be so fortunate to be chosen.

Another excellent opportunity I had here was to run the 26.2-mile Boston Marathon not once, but twice for one of our clients, The Home for Little Wanderers. I have run hundreds of long-distance races since I was in high school, and ran my first of 20 marathons (so far) in Amherst, Massachusetts in 1980. To participate in this historic race for a client, raising funds for such a great cause, was a special treat, a chance to combine my passion for running with my profession in direct response fundraising. Thanks to all my supporters as well as my employer, I was able to raise $2,927 for The Home in 2002 and even more, $3,488, in 2003.

As I mentioned, I also did a lot of traveling on this job. Not just local travel and road trips, but flying to cities like New York, Washington D.C. and Chicago.

One trip in particular stands out to me. We went on a field trip to Murchison, Texas, to visit Cleveland Amory's Black Beauty Ranch. Yes, that Cleveland Amory (the legendary humorist, humanitarian, author, commentator and critic) and that Black Beauty Ranch, a world-renowned animal sanctuary where all kinds of wild animals roam free. I'm talking about antelope, apes, horses, donkeys, lions, tigers and bears. I took a ton of great pictures on this trip, all with a prized possession of mine, a 35-millimeter Canon Rebel camera. No, smartphones with cameras weren't a thing yet.

The miles were adding up, though. All that travel was taking a toll on me. Not that it was that often, but I wasn't particularly fond of it. I didn't mind flying. It was being away from my wife and young children that was a hardship to me. That was also a requirement of the job, one that I clearly had to meet if I wanted to keep myself in good stead at this job.

I was proud to be working at this firm again. It had a stellar reputation in the industry. Locally, too. John, its founder, lived in Franklin, the town in which I was born, and was highly regarded in the community at large and the industry as a whole. Everybody knew, liked and respected John.

Sadly, however, John died suddenly on September 10, 2001.

To say those who knew him were shocked and inconsolable would be an understatement. His passing was a monumental personal and professional loss to countless friends, family members and colleagues. Not only had he built a company known for its success far and wide, he had been heralded as an unparalleled leader in the fundraising field, not to mention an outstanding human being. It was a tragic time for those of us who worked with him, never mind how difficult it must have been for his loved ones.

Then there was September 11, the very next day.

When I arrived at the office that morning, I remember seeing what had happened when I turned on my computer and jumped onto the internet. I remember not knowing what to say or even how to feel. Within minutes, many of us were huddled in a conference room watching the horrible events unfold on television, shedding tears now for both our company's founder and dear friend, as well as our fellow citizens who had just been killed or hurt in the terrorist attacks.

I couldn't have been any more despondent and depressed, worried about everything and grieving for everyone.

Time waits for no one, though. My colleagues and I found ourselves soldiering on through the tough times, shouldering these burdens, taking it one day at a time, rolling with the emotional bumps and bruises, dealing with the doldrums.

It was an especially complicated time to be raising funds. The public was preoccupied with their own health and welfare, the state of the union and the future of our country. On the one hand, philanthropy and benevolence were top of mind. On the other hand, people were worried, stressed, discouraged and distracted.

I did some of my very best writing for clients while I was at this job, though. Not even a question. We were working with some of the biggest brands in the nonprofit industry. I was working with some of the best direct response fundraising professionals in the business. The work was as good for our clients as it was for our egos. We were doing well by doing good.

But digital marketing was calling me. I wanted to be working on more than just direct mail. I had had my taste of the dot-com world at my previous job, and I couldn't forget it. I pictured my future online, not offline, writing email, not direct mail.

It was regrettable that I was feeling this way about moving on. I had an extraordinarily good job here. The creative team I managed couldn't have been friendlier. Same with my colleagues throughout the firm.

Plus, I looked up to Susan, our president, so very, very much. Like John, she was industry-renowned for her expertise and experience in fundraising. She was a remarkably strong leader and a super supportive boss. I had learned so much from working with her. She was such an inspiration to me and everyone else who worked at the firm.

What was I thinking? Why would I be leaving such a great place to work yet again?

A colleague there of mine, Ben, had asked me once what I preferred, fame or fortune. To his amazement and even incredulity, I chose fame. I chose excitement and challenge, risks and thrills, over safe and sound, tried and true. I chose making a name for myself over making more money.

That might explain — at least partially — all my job-hopping. That might explain my thoughts at this time.

There was a religious sanctuary next door to our agency. I would take walks over there often, contemplating my future, taking a few minutes to relax. This shrine was where I would go to get away from the pressure and to make some of my biggest decisions. It was peaceful there, a safe haven.

It was there where I found myself, moments before telling Susan that I was leaving. It was there that I pondered saying goodbye to what should have been my dream job for yet another opportunity, another temptation that I couldn't resist, another attempt at glory and glamour, the needle in the haystack in my long, strange professional journey.

If Susan was surprised, if not disappointed, I could perfectly understand. After all, who could imagine me leaving such a coveted position at a blue-chip company for almost an identical role at a much smaller place with a much longer commute? I would likely be working for lesser-known clients. I would be driving into Boston every day from Sudbury, an hour or so on the road each way. I would be managing only a few others, if that, instead of a dozen or so.

But I had already made up my mind. I was envisioning what I foresaw as the bright lights of the big city, the potential of finding myself higher up the corporate ladder, the promise of being able to write my own blog.

In exchange for how good I felt about being courted by my future employer, though, I was also feeling terribly torn and ambivalent. I had been working there at this job for only a little over two years, but it felt like a lifetime. I was about to leave behind a good, comfortable situation.

One afternoon shortly before my last day there, I closed the door and cried like a big baby in my office. I was worried I was making a big mistake. I was afraid I was about to take one too many chances.

At least this time I wasn't being laid off, like the last time I shed tears on the job about 20 years ago. This was not a problem to worry about. This was a good problem to have. This was an opportunity to take advantage of, and I was grabbing the bull by the horns. At least that's what I told myself.

My colleagues gave me a huge, congratulatory send-off, unintentionally reminding me how much I would be missing — the people, the work, the role itself — as opposed to making me feel good about my decision. They presented me with a big group photo of themselves which they had signed with well wishes. They were like a family to me. I would remember them forever, fondly.

I would also be racked with guilt.

Why I was saying goodbye to them, I couldn't completely fathom. That was the bane of my professional existence. That was the rambling man in me. All I knew was that was a pattern I apparently had to live with; as soon as I became comfortable in one place, I found myself anxious to move on to another place.

Unbridled ambition, misguided intention, ADD, OCD, fear, self-sabotage, doubt, anxiety, goals, manifestations, neurodiversity in some shape or form. Whatever it was, it was a hard, if not impossible habit to break.

LESSON 14 TAKE THE *INITIATIVE*

LESSON 14, TAKE THE INITIATIVE

DARE TO TAKE ON WORK THAT COULD LEAD TO TRANSFORMATIVE CHANGE. SACRIFICE THE HOURS FOR THE GAINS, THE EFFORT FOR THE REWARD. IDENTIFY THE WIN-WIN SITUATIONS WHERE BOTH YOU AND YOUR EMPLOYER ARE REWARDED. OWN THE RESPONSIBILITY, BUT SHARE THE GLORY.

2004 -2005

The beginning of my first blog post in my new position said that the first day on the job here couldn't have gone better, that "it really was, like the U2 song that I woke up to in the morning, a beautiful day." That was the beginning of my life on social media in general. Little did I know then that Facebook, Twitter, YouTube, Instagram and the like would soon follow, but I certainly knew for sure that I loved being able to share news and views with relative autonomy online.

I had already been on LinkedIn for a while. I was actually the 882,759[th] person to join LinkedIn, an early adopter if ever there was one, considering there are over 800,000,000 people on LinkedIn today. I sensed then that communications, including marketing, advertising and PR, was slowly but surely going digital.

That said, the bulk of my job was still writing direct mail. Traditional, old-school marketing. This agency's clients were very similar to those we had had when I worked at Jobs 5 and 13, only smaller. There was a little more variety to what I would be doing there, including more print and collateral, but my focus would be primarily direct response fundraising.

As bad as the commute into Boston from Sudbury was, the office I had was cool.

We were located in the Boston Design Center, now known as the Innovation and Design Building, in the city's historic Seaport District. The building was built by the Department of Defense in 1918, and originally served as a waterside storehouse for the South Boston Army Base. Specifically, my office was located in a narrow, overhead walkway between the Design Center building and the Raymond L. Flynn Black Falcon Terminal, an office that was certainly not lacking in character and charm.

I was full of vim and vigor at this agency. I was the new kid on the block: headstrong, resolved, driven, determined, naïve and blind to what was clearly (in retrospect) an immovable, intractable corporate culture, even though it was such a small, entrepreneurial shop.

"You insulted the whole company when you wrote that email," I was told in no uncertain terms by my boss' number two executive.

Yikes.

I had written a company-wide manifesto, if you will, suggesting that — to paraphrase then presidential contender's Howard Dean's slogan for his political campaign at the time — we embark on a Sleepless Summer campaign to win new business and exceed the expectations of our current client base.

But it wasn't my place, even though I was speaking up with only the best of intentions. Nathaniel was livid.

I was mortified and chagrined, left speechless, standing there all alone with no defense.

That was just one of a few, shall I say awkward, moments there.

There was the time Walter tried to give me a review and I kept interrupting him, saying I didn't need a boss, and certainly not him.

"But I am your boss," he pleaded, "and it's my job to give you a review."

I was acting like I didn't want a job, never mind a review.

I was also upset with one of my new colleagues who had rolled her eyes at me when I suggested she do something a different way.

I was overmatched and underprepared for my new territory and responsibilities.

That was my bad. That was my lesson to be learned the hard way.

I loved writing that blog, though, talking about what we were doing as an agency and what was going on in the worlds of marketing and social media.

That blog connected the agency and me as its author to a much larger universe, the "blogosphere," as it was called at the time, the large, expanding body of other blogs that were being launched during the infancy of social media.

"I am being interviewed by the New York Times," I told my boss.

I could hardly contain my enthusiasm. I could hardly believe it myself. That blog had gotten us attention before, but not from a newspaper by the likes of the Times, the paper that has won more Pulitzer prizes (125 to be exact) than any other.

But Walter's positive reaction was nothing compared to my father-in-law's, to whom the Times was like the Bible.

"My son-in-law is going to be in the Times," he shouted, practically jumping up and down with glee.

If he didn't have faith in me before as the husband of his youngest daughter, he certainly did now.

That new job was the beginning of my blog, the very same blog that I am still writing to this day. Thankfully, I took that initiative. Thankfully, Walter gave me the green light. After all, that blog not only changed my career, it changed my life, opening doors to new opportunities and experiences that I never would have had otherwise.

I loved the variety of work I did in this position. Besides the blog, I wrote plenty of direct mail (consistent with the first 25 years or so of my career) as well as print ads and collateral, mostly for nonprofit organizations.

One of the most creative pieces I worked on there was a wall calendar that we distributed to clients and prospects that included a marketing tip each month. Not only was this thing beautifully designed, it was incredibly clever, something that those on the receiving end really would appreciate.

As I had written in a case study of this award-winning piece…

"This clever, colorful calendar wasn't just memorable and useful, it was designed to trigger a favorable response. Using the latest in variable data-digital printing technology, all three pieces were highly personalized, featuring the recipient's name in big, bold letters. Each month of the calendar featured a tip on how to "take your organization's direct marketing initiatives to the next level," plus a corresponding coupon, good for one free half-hour consultation with [Agency Name]."

But I did a lot more than writing there. I went on sales calls with Walter quite often, helping him reel in new business for the agency. We were a great team, although I have to admit, I wasn't feeling it shortly into my tenure there.

Looking back on my career so far, again, I know I haven't been very patient with my job situations. I haven't stayed very long at any of my stops, which I know could be perceived as job-hopping, or even worse, disloyalty. That was never the case.

Not only am I quite impatient, I am also ambitious to a fault. I can't stay in one place for long. Period. Honestly, I think it's part Attention-Deficit Disorder and part Obsessive-Compulsive Disorder, never mind depression and anxiety. It's just the way I roll as a human being. I get restless very easily. I also get very anxious. Constant movement (literally, in some cases, but also figuratively, emotionally, physically, you name it) is both my salve and my salvation, my weakness and my strength.

There's certainly a strong upside to my tendencies. Because of all this hyperactivity, I am a natural overachiever, always trying to capitalize on my circumstances.

The downside, of course, is that due to my constant proclivity for reinvention, it is probably not easy for others to pin me down. Now you see me, now you don't.

One of the highlights of my time working for Walter was having the chance to present a 60-second promotional message on the agency's behalf at an industry conference. This was a great opportunity for me to demonstrate I was much more than someone who wrote junk mail for a living. This was right up my alley.

I waited at the back of a long line of company representatives, each of whom were fidgety, pacing back and forth, rehearsing their lines and looking at their notes. As was I. We were the chosen ones, like it or not. I liked it. I killed it. This was me reaching above and beyond. This was me feeling better about my contributions to our success.

It was a relatively large audience. I was under a modicum of pressure. It was not something I did for a living except for the occasional speaking gig. It was something I loved doing and probably could have sought opportunities to do more often during my full-time corporate career.

We make decisions. We react to circumstances. We try hard. We do our best.

But the fact is that we can easily end up doing something we didn't plan to do for all the days of our lives. We can change our minds. We can hem. We can haw. We can punt. We can turn everything around. We can flip. We can reverse course. But we often keep our heads down and go full speed ahead in the direction we set out upon when were too young to know better.

I have always been stuck between feeling like I am not good enough and feeling like I am selling myself short. I am both decisive and hesitant, fast and slow, good and bad. If I was successful, I used to say to myself, I would have more money, own a big company, maybe even be retired. This wouldn't be my first book, this would be my 10th book. This wouldn't be about working here, there and everywhere, this would be about working at one great company and doing many great things all the days of my life.

I tried to do great things at this agency, as hard as I tried everywhere else. In some cases, I succeeded, but the fact that I left after such a relatively short period of time certainly places an asterisk on this stint, certainly in any conventionalist's mind.

That's a shame though, if that's the case. My feeling is that I have gotten the equivalent of a different marketing education at every place I've worked.

Who knows more about marketing? Is it the individual who has worked in only one place for 40 years, or the one who has worked in in as many places as I have over the years?

I'll stand by my experience any day. I'll stand by what I did at this agency, Job 14, too. I gave it everything I had, working long hours, writing, directing, managing, leading and trying hard to be the best I could be at the time.

Like everywhere else I have worked, I was hoping that this would be it, that this would be my professional home for a very long time, if not forever.

Can you feel the disappointment I have felt over the years? The loss? The hurt? My fault or not, it's palpable. It's real. Saying goodbye time and again is heartbreaking. Leaving people — especially when they've become friends to you, not simply colleagues — and places in the rearview mirror is painful.

Thank you, Walter, for being the only boss in the history of my career who actually asked me to stay, not leave (he put that in writing, too, by the way, in all caps), who asked me to change my mind and finish what I started, not give up mid-stream. Hindsight is 20-20. You are such a good, good guy, Walter. I didn't deserve such a ridiculously awesome boss as you.

All blog posts in this chapter, Chapter 14, were written by Bob Cargill for the blog, A Fine Kettle of Fish, which was the blog founded and written by Bob at Yellowin Direct Marketing that became his blog (eventually renamed to A New Marketing Commentator and now simply residing at thebobcargill.com) once he left the company.

SALESMAN, FUNDRAISER, ACTOR, MYSTIC

A growing percentage of our business here is rooted in the world of higher education, either helping development officers raise funds or working with alumni associations to grow their membership files. If you're familiar with agency parlance, you'll know what I mean when I say this is one of our strongest vertical markets, an offering we've already established as one of a handful of our core competencies. We've run successful campaigns so far for clients such as Ohio University, the University of Texas and Southern Methodist University, just to name a few, which has led to a number of new engagements recently, including the University of Houston and Florida State University. As a creative guy, I couldn't be happier with these assignments. Each one is a step back in time for me, a blissful reminder of days gone by, when I was just an optimistic, young student in search of my own bright future. Each one takes my imagination to another corner of the country — to another whole world, really — where, on some beautiful campus somewhere, the wide-eyed innocence of youth is introduced to the rigors of academics and the complexities of real life. This is what I enjoy so much about my role as a direct mail copywriter. I'm a salesman. I'm a fundraiser. But I'm also an actor, putting myself in the shoes of my signatory. And I'm part mystic, too, asking myself how would I feel if I were on the receiving end of my appeal.

◾ DROP US A LINE

Keeping a blog is a remarkably simple, inexpensive way to build a community of friends and colleagues. In our case, not only is A Fine Kettle of Fish a surprisingly valuable communication channel, but it also allows us to put a personality on the agency, giving us a forum to share our knowledge, exhibit our creativity and hold forth on matters of — ideally — mutual general interest. Word has it that there are more than several million blogs in existence worldwide, but I've only been able to find a handful that are being published by marketing communications agencies. H-m-m-m... Part of me realizes the jury's still out on their viability as a business application, and that many folks are playing the game of wait-and-see. Okay. I can appreciate their sense of prudence. But on the other hand, I'm thinking these guys could be missing the boat. After all, isn't true direct marketing all about initiating a one-to-one dialogue with a mass audience (oxymoronic concept aside)? "Listen to the murmur of your market." That's what Don Jackson writes on page 116 of "2,239 Tested Secrets for Direct Marketing Success," the book he put together with Denny Hatch in 1998. He tells readers: "Create feedback loops in your database environment so that you can record what your customers and prospects are saying about your products, your service, your company and your competition. There is no more valuable source of information." Exactly. This blog is one such "feedback loop." It's one way of interlocking the circle of good people who visit us through our Web site — and establishing mutually beneficial relationships with each and every one of them. It's, well, A Fine Kettle of Fish. So please, don't hesitate to drop us a line.

89

EITHER THEN OR NEVER

If I were to look back on my career so far, a defining moment in time for me was the summer of 1990, when I decided to fly solo as a creative director and join the ranks of the self-employed. For the next seven years, I kept myself busy defining and developing my brand as a direct marketer — not just writing copy, but working closely with a pool of designers and even closer with my clients, all the while realizing, like a parachutist about to jump, that this is what it's like to look destiny in the eyes. But having emerged from the experience far better for the wear, I can't help but wish for every entrepreneur — for every budding professional, really — such an incredible odyssey, such a rare opportunity to challenge your will and test your mettle. Cargill Creative was a "virtual" agency with unlimited potential but resources that were only so deep. Schooled as a creative, I recast myself out of necessity as an account executive, a traffic manager, a salesman and an accountant, too. Occasionally I had enough money in the coffers to employ an additional writer, but for the better part of this gig it was just me, myself and I, the accidental principal who wore all the hats, the chief, cook and bottle washer. The hours were long, the responsibilities were endless, but the upside of being my own boss was the autonomy and freedom, and my professional inhibitions ran wild. It's no coincidence that during this stretch of new found glory I explored options that might otherwise not have been available to me, throwing myself into three organizations — Toastmasters, The New England Direct Marketing Association and The MetroWest Leadership Academy — that, collectively, would have a long-term impact on not just my career, but also my growth as an individual. Call it ambition. Call it survival. Call it biting off more than I could chew (well, almost). But clearly I was refusing to be intimidated by any unfounded fears of failure, knowing full well that much of what I was doing I was doing either then or never.

THE BRILLIANCE TO WHICH WE ASPIRE

Thumbing through the latest issue of Rolling Stone magazine last week, an ad for eBay Motors — smack, dab in between the "Correspondence" and "Rock & Roll" sections — stopped me dead in my tracks.

An extraordinarily simple, no-frills composition, it uses a story about "Brothers John and Tom [who] want a great way to sell their cars" to illustrate the benefits of peddling wheels on eBay versus the old standby, the classifieds. After seven days, John, who uses eBay, "sells his car for a great price," while Tom, who went the old-school route, finds his "ad is used as litter box lining."

It's hip, funny and irreverent, sure, but it's also textbook in formula, drawing on a case study of two young men and employing fear tactics to drive (no pun intended) the point home — not unlike a legendary Wall Street Journal direct mail package written by Martin Conroy three decades earlier.

But Conroy's story about another two young men would be nearly impossible to top. After all, his story was only recently dethroned as the newspaper's control after a 29-year reign, and has been heralded by many as the single most successful ad ever. Yes, ever.

In his story, the protagonists "graduated from the same college. They were very much alike, these two young men. Both had been better than average students, both were personable and both — as young college graduates are — were filled with ambitious dreams for the future. Recently, these men returned to their college for their 25th reunion. They were still very much alike. Both were happily married. Both had three children. And both, it turned out, had gone to work for the same Midwestern service company after graduation and were still there. But there was a difference. One of the men was a manager of a small department of that company. The other was its president."

91

Of course, the implication — and the author draws it masterfully — is that the more successful of the two young men read The Wall Street Journal.

That is the brilliance of Martin Conroy. That is the brilliance that captured the emotions of countless would-be subscribers to the tune of an estimated $2 billion in sales. And that is the brilliance to which every direct marketer — including the creative team behind the eBay Motors ad, I'm sure — aspires.

A BIG LESSON IN MARKETING

The success of any advertising or direct marketing campaign depends on a coalescence of elements, not the least of which are the motif of the creative and the timing of the launch. If you can tie those two together, you're likely to be sitting pretty.

For example, take the Sunday newspaper insert I received recently from Target, which prides itself on selling quality, stylish merchandise at reasonable prices. Scheduled to arrive in-home about a week before the first day of school, it was obviously designed by the retailer to look like a classic composition notebook — ruled pages, marble red cover and all.

But the "back to school" theme doesn't stop there. This bold, eye-catching, 8-1/2" X 11" insert is divided into three two-page spreads — one each for middle school, high school and elementary school — each of which features a selection of obligatory, age-appropriate school supplies, clothes and gear.

But wait — it gets better. We're not just talking back packs, calculators, plaid skirts and denim blazers here. No, you have to give extra credit to Target for using this opportunity to cross-promote Take Charge of Education, its community relations and credit initiative which, since 1997, has donated over $100 million to schools across the country.

"Every time you use your Target Visa or Target Guest Card, Target donates up to 1% of the purchase amount to the K-12 school of your choice," reads the plug.

And as if the creative team behind this masterpiece hadn't already pulled out enough stops, they added one final flourish on the inside back cover: Above a picture of the ubiquitous Target Bullseye Dog are these three parting words — "See. Spot. Save."

Wow! Clearly, the folks at Target know much more than just the A, B, C's of promoting sales of their goods. In one small notebook, they teach a big lesson in marketing.

◣ THE ART OF CLIENT SERVICE

If it wasn't for a pair of brown leather cowboy boots, my career in direct marketing may have taken a different turn a long time ago.

The year was 1984, and I had a great job as a copywriter at RCA Direct Marketing. But when a friend told me about another job as an account executive at Grey Direct, my youth and ambition got the best of me. I applied for it. The interview went well, but word got back to me afterwards that I hadn't dressed the part. Sure, I was wearing the requisite Brooks Brothers blue pinstripe suit, but my feet were covered in Dingo boots instead of classic wing tip shoes. My bad!

Today, of course, I would like to believe the fact that I didn't land this new job was a blessing in disguise. After all, I stayed the course as a copywriter and eventually "happily" grew into my present role as a creative director. However, ever since that bad, fateful interview two decades ago, not only have I always worn oxfords to the office, but I have also had an affinity with those on the client services side of the house. I don't know, maybe it has something to do with the axiom, "one of the best ways to understand someone is to walk a mile in his or her shoes."

Given that spirit, I have always made a point of understanding what it takes to be a good AE, going so far as to read recently "The Art of Client Service, 54 Things Every Advertising & Marketing Professional Should Know." Written by Robert Solomon, President and CEO of the New York office of Rapp Collins Worldwide, this 168-page book is really the definitive guide to everything anyone would need to know about client service and then some.

Broken down into three parts (The Work, Relationships, Style and Substance), Solomon uses both successes and failures to make his points about looking at creative ("When you are in front of the client, never throw the work, or your colleagues, under the bus."), to running a meeting ("Once a meeting is underway, the goal should be to make it as short as possible. Get it done so everyone can get out and do the work."), to communication ("A commitment without consultation ignores the collaborative nature of making advertising. It pays no respect to the people you work with. Besides, you might not be able to deliver on your commitment."), to "apropos of this post" style and substance ("Looking good is just one more detail in a business that is all about details. So why not get this one right?").

Okay, so that's one detail I got wrong back in the day. I wore boots when I should have worn shoes. At the time, I felt bad about making such a foolish mistake. But today, I can't help but feel good about such a momentous quirk of fate. After all, I think life on the creative side "so far" has suited me just fine.

■ ONE OF THE HABITS OF HIGHLY EFFECTIVE MARKETERS

All experienced copywriters know how advantageous it is to establish common ground from the get-go with those on the receiving end of our messages and offers. Whether we're selling products and services or raising funds for charitable organizations, like ambassadors of goodwill, it behooves us to speak the same language as the constituencies before us, it pays to strike a chord to which almost everyone can relate.

For instance, in the early '90s I wrote a direct mail package for *Science News* magazine that featured the following copy on the outside envelope:

"Electricity so powerful it shocks a heart-attack victim back to life...

Whales so hungry they take a bite out of the beach...

Grasshoppers so smart they change coats to beat the heat...

And other things that will make you go hmmm..."

If that last line sounds familiar to you now, just imagine how many people took notice then when they saw it on the envelope. "Things that make you go hmmm" just so happened to be the name of a hit song at the time by C&C Music Factory as well as a popular skit on a syndicated, late-night talk show hosted by Arsenio Hall. It was almost universally recognized, a clever, common expression that couldn't help but command attention.

I couldn't have gotten away with using it just for that reason, though. That would have been gratuitous and superficial and possibly even ineffective. The fact is that *Science News* really is full of things that make you go hmmm, so I was simply calling attention to its Unique Selling Proposition (USP) with powerful, loaded language that was already embedded in the vernacular of the mainstream, using three of the magazine's most fascinating stories to sell subscriptions.

And sell subscriptions is what this package did, bringing in thousands of orders over the course of the several years it reigned as a control for *Science News*, and being honored by the New England Direct Marketing Association with a first place award as a result.

That was more than ten years ago.

What conjures up such fond professional memories is an ad I saw just a couple of weeks ago in the May 9 issue of ADWEEK for The New York Times that adopted the same technique I used on behalf of Science News, leveraging the lexicon of popular culture as a way to build rapport. Promoting the new Business Day, "enhanced business coverage with a specific focus each day," The Times used a play on the title of Stephen Covey's best-selling book, "The 7 Habits of Highly Effective People," as the headline for this ad.

"The 7 Habits of Highly Effective Business People:

They read it Monday.

They read it Tuesday.

They read it Wednesday.

They read it Thursday.

They read it Friday.

They read it Saturday.

They read it Sunday.

The New York Times introduces the new Business Day."

Now that's powerful copy, the perfect marriage of concept and product, creative and message, all buttoned up and good to go.

And unlike the copy I used to promote the circulation of Science News (I had to assume potential readers would have at least heard of C&C Music Factory and Arsenio Hall, admittedly a big stretch when you factored in the different demographics), who among the The Times' constituency isn't familiar with Stephen Covey's book and wouldn't be able to relate to such a riveting, relevant headline?

Such fine distinctions aside, like my line of thinking way back when, the creative team behind this ad for Business Day obviously realized just how powerful it is to use double entendres and other such word plays to associate their advertising with what's most popular in culture today. You might say they practiced one of the habits of highly effective marketers. And for that they deserve kudos, if not their audience's, well, business.

LESSON 15

IT'S A HARD, BUMPY RIDE

LESSON 15, IT'S A HARD, BUMPY RIDE
UNLESS YOU'RE VERY FORTUNATE, CHANCES ARE YOUR CAREER IS NOT GOING TO BE EASY. THERE ARE PLENTY OF UPHILL CHALLENGES DOWN THE ROAD. PREPARE FOR THE UNEXPECTED BECAUSE YOU NEVER KNOW WHAT'S AROUND THE NEXT CORNER.

2005-2006

Once again, I found myself working in the attic. Like the last time I was suddenly solo, I was suddenly wondering what was going to happen next in my professional journey. Only this time around, I wasn't laid off. This was my choice. I had been in control of my own destiny. This time around wasn't for long, either. After freelancing for a while, I was quickly offered another full-time job with another small agency, one located in Duxbury, Massachusetts, an upscale community on the south shore of Boston.

I have covered a lot of ground in the agency world in the eastern portion of Massachusetts.

This was going to be another long commute, over 50 miles each way, but it was not going to be as crazy as driving into the city every day. Plus, they said I could work from home one day a week, which was greatly appreciated and would go a long way toward alleviating the stress of being in the car so often.

This was yet another job seemingly right in my wheelhouse. Writing direct mail. Helping to put together the agency's website. Working on a series of self-promotional ads, both print and online, to help get the word out about the agency's ridiculously awesome services.

I had my own office, a big plus. I even had the pleasure of being able to get in a nice workout after work, running to the famous Powder Point Bridge and back, passing by the beach, the water and the mansions along the coast. It was a beautiful way of ending the day before I got in my car for the long drive home.

Everyone who worked at this agency was wicked smart and super nice. Their expertise and experience in direct response fundraising ran deep. Thought leaders, strategists, consultants, account executives, designers, project managers; these were true team players and top-notch industry professionals who worked seamlessly together. I was proud — and lucky — to be working here.

Writing copy for our website was a lot of fun. Writing so-called self-promotional work, whether it was for my own personal brand or my employer's, has always come naturally to me, so this was a great opportunity to do what I do best. They also had me write a new brochure for the agency as well as a few ads. These are still some of the best-looking pieces of work in my portfolio.

The direct mail I worked on during my time at this shop was top-shelf as well. These were exemplary fundraising packages, tried-and-true campaigns that incorporated very best practices to ensure optimum results. We focused as much on the science of direct mail as the art. We concentrated on not just meeting, but exceeding client expectations.

Blogging was something I continued to do on the side. Call it moonlighting. Call it a passion. Call it an obsession. Whatever you call it, I was confident that it was something that was not only going to be part of the industry's future, but my future as well. The opportunity to self-publish had finally presented itself to those of us content creators who were starving for readers and attention. I was not going to stop taking advantage of it. I didn't necessarily envision my blog posts being incorporated into a book one day, but I did realize, that I was writing a documentary of not just my career but the evolution of marketing.

Unfortunately, my days on the job here at this blue-chip agency, Job 15, were numbered. I had been a contract hire, so I had known that I likely wasn't going to be there for a long time.

It had been a stellar stint, a heck of a ride. Everybody there had been so nice to me. I was thankful to have had the opportunity to work at this agency. Very thankful. They were really good people who had given me a really good job.

I can still hear my car's tires slowly peeling themselves away from the gravel parking lot outside the agency headquarters as I write these words. It was my last day there. It was time to hit the highway.

Gone was yet another opportunity for me to realize my professional dreams. Gone was that office. Gone was a great team of ridiculously awesome colleagues. Gone was that job.

I found myself on the road again, literally, with yet another career disappointment disappearing in the rear-view mirror. There I went back towards Boston, up route three north on my way home to Sudbury. There I went once again with my tail between my legs.

All blog posts in this chapter, Chapter 15, were written by Bob Cargill for the blog, A Fine Kettle of Fish, which was the blog founded and written by Bob at Yellowin Direct Marketing that became his blog (eventually renamed to A New Marketing Commentator and now simply residing at thebobcargill.com) once he left the company.

THE POWER OF LOYALTY MARKETING

Every shopper likes to belong, to feel like an insider, to get a good deal that can't be had anywhere else. At least, those are the cravings that retailers are counting on — and playing to — by asking their customers to use so-called loyalty cards, those small pieces of plastic so many of us have been conditioned like sheep to carry around in our wallets or on our key chains.

I don't know about you, but I have a handful of them, three for groceries alone (Stop & Shop, Shaw's and Price Chopper), one for books (Barnes & Noble) and one for, well, this and that (CVS/ Pharmacy).

And while I sometimes feel like I'm being subjected to undue scrutiny when asked to produce one of these cards at the register, like a groupie with a backstage pass, I'm always happy to oblige. To me, the benefit of identifying myself to a clerk (okay, to a computer database) in what some might characterize as an Orwellian moment far outweighs the hassle.

Sure, there are those who dismiss such a business transaction as too "big brother"-like, worrying about the potential misuse of private, personal data for unfair and disproportionate commercial gain. But obviously I'm not one of them.

The truth is that loyalty cards are a great way for marketers to monitor buying patterns and forge long-lasting, mutually-beneficial relationships with their target constituencies. In exchange for handsome discounts on products and services, or a certain number of points which can be used towards future purchases, they give the issuing establishments a way of tracking your behavior as a consumer and, thus, stocking their aisles accordingly.

Take the Hallmark Gold Crown Card, for instance, which my wife, Barbara, dutifully keeps in her purse. Hallmark uses this card to track — and thank her for — how much she spends on its products. Over time, her points accumulate and she receives what the company refers to as "reward certificates," each one worth at least a couple dollars off her next Hallmark purchase.

One of these "certificates" arrived in the mail recently along with a birthday card addressed to Barbara — yes, a real Hallmark birthday card, canary yellow envelope, gold-embossed wafer seal and all — from The Paper Store in Sudbury, perhaps my wife's favorite place to shop, located just a few miles from our house.

To say she was surprised — albeit pleasantly — to receive such a generous offer disguised as a birthday card would be an understatement.

What's not so surprising, however, is that such loyalty marketing tactics are incredibly effective. After all, not only does Hallmark have my wife's address, it knows where and when she shops for greeting cards as well as how faithful she is to its brand.

Talk about a captive audience!

But my better half isn't the only one in my house on the Hallmark file. The fact that I use my Extra Care card so often at CVS/Pharmacy, another store in Sudbury, means I get a lot of direct mail from this chain's corporate headquarters. That doesn't mean I was prepared, however, for the brilliantly executed, cooperative *promotional piece I received last year (and wrote about here in my blog) before my own birthday on behalf of Hallmark's Shoe-box line of cards.*

I like to buy a handful of cards at a time, and I had just recently gone on a binge. So not only did CVS (with a little help from Hallmark) have the mailing lists and sales proposition down pat, but the timing was right, too.

Let's not overlook the creative presentation, either. Not unlike the aforementioned piece of mail my wife received from Hallmark, inside a faux hand-addressed envelope were several coupons for Shoebox cards nested inside an actual, life-size birthday card that read as follows:

"It may not be your birthday, but we just couldn't wait to show you this great card! It's from the new Shoebox collection at your local CVS store. Come on down for a look, and bring these exclusive coupons along. They're our way of saying thank you for being one of our most valued customers."

Yup, one of their most valued customers. That's me. That's me and my wife, too, not to mention practically everyone and his or her uncle, all of us card-carrying converts to the power of loyalty marketing, whether we realize it or not.

IN DEFENSE OF RUBBER WRISTBANDS AS A FUND-RAISING TOOL

In the latest issue of Details magazine (June/July 2005, p. 99), columnist Jonathan Sabin plays the devil's advocate and argues that rubber wristbands — such as those ubiquitous yellow ones that have helped the Lance Armstrong Foundation raise so much money for such a good cause — should be banned.

Who would have thought that one man's solution to cancer prevention and survivorship would be another man's problem with marketing and philanthropy?

"Today nearly 50 million are looped around self-righteous wrists as the cheesy trinkets metastasize like the cancers they're supposed to help cure," writes Sabin, taking an unseemly, cheap shot — in my opinion — at not just one of the most popular charitable organizations going right now, but at the business of direct response fundraising as a whole.

In the same article, Sabin claims "the problem is that we've become a nation of philanthropic exhibitionists."

I can think of worse things to show off than one's benevolence.

Indeed, with all due respect to Jonathan Sabin, I think the real problem is the fact that there is so much disease and poverty and injustice in the world.

I think the real problem is that there are not enough people who are willing to give selflessly of themselves on behalf of others less fortunate.

If Americans take pride in their generosity and are wearing these wristbands as status symbols, so be it.

If fundraisers have a way of bringing in more charitable gifts, good for them and their beneficiaries, good for those who are counting on them to provide as much financial assistance and emotional relief as possible.

Why rain on Lance Armstrong's seemingly endless parade of inspiration, courageousness and goodwill?

Sure, many people, young and old alike, enjoy wearing these wristbands as much because they're a hip, new fashion statement as a way to help others. But that doesn't matter.

What matters is that by offering such a cool tchotchke, nonprofit organizations of all kinds are able to amass more individual contributions (because the demand for wristbands is so strong), a higher average gift (because people are willing to give more when they're getting something extra in return) and a glut of free publicity and promotion (because such body ornaments are attracting so much attention).

What matters is that more money is being raised to help more people in need, people who really couldn't care less if donors want to wear silly rubber wristbands in their honor, as long as the reason for this jewelry gives them a reason to hope and believe in the future.

THE NEW ENGLAND DIRECT MARKETING ASSOCIATION'S BRAVE NEW CONFERENCE BLOG

I'm pleased to announce that the New England Direct Marketing Association has just launched a blog to help promote its upcoming conference, NEDMA '06, It's a Brave New World. And, in addition to my position as co-chair of the conference, I couldn't be more excited — or, some might say, fanatical — to be taking on the responsibilities of moderating this blog.

Yes, like any blog, it'll be a labor of love for all involved, but the truth is that using a blog as an online propagation tool should almost be a requirement for anyone staging a major conference amidst today's new marketing landscape.

Not only will a blog enable NEDMA to post key news and information on the fly, but it'll also allow us to engage our different audiences — sponsors, exhibitors, speakers and attendees — early and often. The blog will work both ways, benefiting not just the senders but those on the receiving end, too.

As I wrote in my first post on the NEDMA conference blog:

"Yes, this is your conference. And this is your blog. As much as we'd like you to be a frequent visitor here (you can subscribe by entering your email address in the FeedBlitz box below), we also hope you'll contribute to the conversation by giving us your honest feedback every now and then on everything conference-related. To do so, simply click on the comment link underneath the post of your choice and write to your heart's content. It's easy to do and will take just a few minutes of your time. By talking back to us in such a manner, you'll be playing a significant role in helping us develop this blog into a community of like-minded direct marketers, people who not only enjoy what they do for a living, but who enjoy doing it with each other."

And that's really what a blog is all about, isn't it? Bringing constituents — who, in this day and age, are increasingly stretched thin — together for a common cause.

▌GREY DIRECT'S LAWRENCE KIMMEL RALLIES DIRECT MARKETERS

Kudos to Lawrence M. Kimmel, chairman and CEO of Grey Direct, for speaking his mind and rallying the direct marketing troops to stand up and be counted — post haste.

"I'm frustrated," writes Kimmel in the November 7 edition of DM News. "As direct marketers, this is our moment to shine. The world of advertising is in radical transformation. The pillars of the ad business — 30-second commercials, radio advertising, magazines, newspapers and even direct mail — are losing their effectiveness. Viewership, readership and response rates are declining while costs continue to rise. Consumers are rejecting

conventional intrusion advertising en mass and gravitating to in-clusion advertising: keyword search, e-mail marketing, targeted online communications. Marketers are demanding greater accountability and better ROI."

"Yet it doesn't seem as if direct marketers are doing enough to champion our cause. We are not leading the marketing community," adds Kimmel.[1]

You can say that again.

In my opinion, the direct marketing industry needs to invest in its own future — now — or else. Far too many of us are preoccupied with direct mail — placing an inordinate amount of faith in the long-term viability of this age-old medium — and view the Internet as more of a threat than an opportunity.

We're not seeing the forest for the trees.

As an industry, instead of using new technologies and channels to leverage the strategies and principles of direct, we're running the risk of getting beaten at our own game by not just those in advertising, but by any and all communications professionals who have a vested interest in marketing in the new millennium.

"Direct marketers hold marketing's Holy Grail. The world just needs to catch up," says Kimmel later on in this same DM News article.

I couldn't agree with him more. But what's frightening — and ironic — is that the world may be catching up to us faster than we are to it.

THE DING HEARD 'ROUND THE MARKETING WORLD

It's not the first branded desktop application to be used for marketing purposes, but it has certainly struck a chord with con-sumers and marketers alike.

107

DING, a simple, little desktop application used by Southwest Airlines to stimulate more ticket sales, has worked so well for the Dallas-based company that it's only a matter of time before others follow suit — if they haven't already — and launch similar initiatives of their own.

In an article in DM News on December 5, 2005, Christine Blank wrote, "Online research firm Compete Inc., Boston, found that DING users are 45 percent more likely to book tickets through Southwest than the average visitor to Southwest.com. Sales driven through the services are estimated at $60 million a year."

"More than 900,000 consumers have downloaded the free application, which sits in the computer user's system tray and delivers daily offers exclusive to DING users, since it launched in February [of 2005]," according to Blank.[2]

And then, less than a month after the DM News article appeared, the Boston Herald reported that office supplies retail behemoth Staples "is spreading its marketing efforts from the television screen to the computer screen after launching another installment yesterday [January 1, 2006] of the Easy Button series complete with a downloadable icon for computer desktops."

"Staples' logo joins a myriad of marketers jockeying for position on computer screens," wrote Jesse Noyes in a January 2 Herald article ("Getting in Your Face, Desktop Marketing Taking Off"). "Desktop applications, ranging from games and online links to wallpapers and screen savers, are gaining popularity with brands looking to build awareness among consumers that extends beyond the traditional 30-second TV spot."[3]

Reinventing the Wheel

Sounds like somebody's been reading Joe Jaffe's excellent, new book, "Life After the 30-Second Spot," in which the "new marketing" consultant warns the old-schoolers among us that they had better adapt to the rapidly changing times and reinvent the wheel — or else.

In this case, Staples (like Southwest) is clearly ahead of the curve, bringing its phenomenally popular Easy Button campaign to a computer screen near you. Once downloaded, the button will link customers directly to the Staples Web site, where they can shop online for all the office products they need.

Desktop marketing such as this is the concept of permission marketing — the process of promoting the sales of products and services to prospects who have explicitly agreed in advance to receive marketing messages — squared.

After all, what could be better than having your constituents not just willingly, but actively — proactively, even — participating in the sales process?

Engendering Brand Loyalty

A branded desktop application can go a long way towards engendering loyalty among your target audience and increasing their lifetime value — not just incrementally, but many times over — to you.

Think how much time most of us spend every single day in front of our computer screens, and how we're practically beholden to the applications that have been granted a permanent residence there.

AOL. Internet Explorer. Norton AntiVirus. QuickTime. Adobe Reader. Imagine what it would be like for your brand to keep company with these desktop icons. (Never mind desktop or permission marketing — this is "right in front of your face" marketing!) Imagine how you could use your own DING or Easy Button.

If you were a magazine publisher, you could let your readers know when it was time to renew their subscriptions.

If you were a nonprofit organization, you could get in touch with your donors instantly when disaster — or any kind of emergency — struck.

If you were a retailer, you could notify shoppers when you were having a sale.

If you were a bank, you could warn customers when their balances were running low.

And if you were a blogger like me, you could rest assured knowing that your subscribers would know when you've written another new post.

Your own DING or Easy Button would serve as a virtual alarm clock for your audience, a Pavlovian-like call-and-response tool.

Okay, so getting people to download and click on your own desktop application would probably not be that easy. But, like it or not, in this day and age, all of us marketing, advertising and PR pros should be at least thinking like those who thought of DING and the Easy Button — or else.

INSTEAD OF THE BLACK DOOR, IT'S A NEW BLOG

Like Debbie Weil (a highly regarded online marketing consultant specializing in new media strategies), I couldn't feel more strongly that fear is what's keeping many Fortune 500 companies from staking a rightful — and long overdue — claim in the blogosphere.

To blog or not to blog is largely a top-down, C-level decision, and those in the front offices, executive suites and boardrooms of corporate America are typically conservative and cautious about trying almost anything new.

With that said, I'm reminded of a parable I've heard many times before (which you can read in its entirety here) about a spy who had been captured by the enemy and sentenced to death. To make a long story short, the condemned man was given the choice between the firing squad and the black door, and he ultimately chose the former because he was so afraid of the latter, which represented the unknown.

Here's how I think this story would go if it were about business today instead of war...

A New Blog (A Parable)

Let me tell you a story. It's about a CEO who, because he had been unsuccessful in positioning his company as a leader in the marketplace, was about to be dismissed by his board of directors. The board, however, permitted the beleaguered executive to choose between being fired and publishing a new blog.

As the moment of termination drew near, the board ordered the CEO to be brought before them to receive the hapless man's decision. It was not an easy decision, and the executive hesitated, but he soon made it known that he preferred to be fired. Not long thereafter, a few tears and good cries around the water cooler announced that the bold decision to let the CEO go had been fulfilled.

The company's marketing director then turned to her assistant and said, "You see how it is with CEOs. They will always prefer the known way to the unknown. It is characteristic of most C-level executives to be afraid of the undefined. And yet he was given a choice!"

"What lies beyond the launch of a new blog?" asked the assistant.

"Transparency," replied the marketing director, "and I've seen only a few corporate Americans brave enough to communicate that way."

Now, there are two messages to this story.

The first, of course, is that the average business man or woman will often choose a familiar means of communications, even if it is undesirable, over an unknown way, which might represent a wonderful opportunity.

And second, that few among us in the business world are brave enough to choose transparency.

I'm not saying that corporate America should stop using the traditional press release, newsletters, direct mail, email and Web sites to get the word out — not by any means. But those of us in business — especially the business of marketing, advertising and public relations — should at least question the usual tools of the trade and challenge the status quo.

Just because it's familiar doesn't mean it's effective, or even the right thing to do — especially in this day and age.

Oh sure, you're probably saying to yourself, "If I were the CEO, I would have chosen to publish a new blog. I would have had nothing to lose. Getting fired is not going to help anyone's career!"

But actually faced with the choice, would you really? How many times in the last year or two have we passed up the chance to launch a blog because we tend to cling so fiercely to any number of more conventional ways of communicating with our customers, prospects and industry peers?

Think about it. How many times during the course of our careers have bold, new ways of communicating been introduced to us that later on proved to be gainful? Each of them — like a blog — was a new platform which we eventually used to communicate better than ever before with those who mean the most to us. But at the time, due to apprehension and fear, we may have settled on a more comfortable method of communications.

It is good to remember that it is often those things we worry about and are afraid of most as business men and women that turn out to be blessings in disguise for our careers and companies.

I'm sure many of you might be reluctant to establish a presence in the blogosphere. To communicate in such a timely, comprehensive manner. To engage your constituents in such open, honest dialogue.

But once you do, will it not add greater freedom — and, ultimately, profits — to your lives as professionals? For many of you, I'm sure, blogging will be the beginning of not just a new way of communicating, but a new era of success.

So I urge all of you C-level executives to not resist change, to not fear the unknown and to not be afraid to launch a new corporate blog today.

HOW TO SUBSCRIBE TO THE NEDMA CONFERENCE BLOG — AND MAYBE WIN A $10 STARBUCKS CARD FOR THE EFFORT

As you may recall, I announced here in January that the New England Direct Marketing Association had launched a blog to help promote its upcoming conference, NEDMA '06, It's a Brave New World.

I also told you that, in addition to my position as co-chair of this conference, I couldn't be more excited to be taking on the responsibilities of moderating this new blog.

"Yes, like any blog, it'll be a labor of love for all involved, but the truth is that using a blog as an online propagation tool should almost be a requirement for anyone staging a major conference amidst today's new marketing landscape," I wrote in this space some six weeks ago.

Well, so far, so good. If I do say myself, I believe we have a pretty awesome blog up and running on behalf of NEDMA '06, and what

I posted on it today will hopefully attract a slew of new subscribers who will feel the same way.

"As a subscriber, you'll know whenever the blog has been updated with new information without ever having to actually go to it. It'll come to you," I wrote just a couple of hours ago, thinking it would make sense to explain to our readers the benefits of subscribing to the blog, as opposed to simply reading it.

I also took the time to define RSS, or Really Simple Syndication:

"This is a way for you to subscribe to this blog — and as many others as you like — through an instantaneous feed brought to you by a feed reader (or aggregator) such as Bloglines.

"At first, RSS may sound confusing, but it's really not. And many online marketing experts say it's the wave of the future, so it makes a lot of sense to at least become familiar with it.

"RSS means both the sender and receiver don't have to worry about the filters that can inadvertently block legitimate emails from reaching their destination.

"RSS makes it possible for you to receive all — and only — the content you want, when you want it, where you want it."

Finally, I told our audience about a special Starbucks Card giveaway:

"As an incentive for you to become a subscriber to this blog sooner rather than later, we're going to give away two $10 Starbucks Cards — one to a reader who subscribes through FeedBlitz and the other to someone who subscribes through Bloglines between the time of this post and 5 PM EST on Monday, March 6."

"To qualify for this drawing, however, you must let us know before the deadline that you've subscribed for the first time by sending an email to Cargill123@aol.com that includes the day and time you became a subscriber and whether you used FeedBlitz or Bloglines as well as your name, company name, mailing address and phone number. We'll announce the two winners here next week. Good luck!"

▌USING DIRECT MAIL TO LAND A NEW JOB

If you've ever been between jobs, you know how much of a challenge it is to stand out in a crowd of those who are ambitiously jockeying for the same gig.

After all, chances are you're just one of dozens, if not hundreds, with relatively similar credentials in line for that one plum position.

And unless you know someone in a corner office who can grant you the inside track, the odds of your resume getting past the gatekeepers and in the hands of the top dog are slim to none, never mind getting your foot in the door for an interview.

With that said, in addition to going about my new job search in all the usual ways — posting my resume on online job boards such as Monster and Talent Zoo, mining Craigslist for that rare golden opportunity, speaking to a slew of professional recruiters and touching base with practically everyone I know in the business — I thought I would do for myself what I've been doing for clients for so long and put together my own little direct mail campaign, asking for a meeting with those whom I would like to work for in the worst way.

Of course, a simple letter alone just wasn't going to cut it. A prospective employer wouldn't stand for anything less than a solicitation out of the ordinary from a creative guy like me. Not only did I need to come up with a compelling offer, but I also needed to present it in a refreshingly different way.

A Cup of Coffee to Wake up My Audience

Given my desire to have a face-to-face meeting with each of my prospects, I settled on a Starbucks Card as a means of coaxing them into sitting down for a cup of coffee with me.

But the strategy for commanding my audience's attention didn't stop there. I wanted to speak to those on the receiving end of this unique, self-promotional campaign at a level they would appreciate — not just as some guy looking for a job, but as a knowledgeable industry peer. My appeal needed to be relevant to the reader, not simply self-serving. The last thing I wanted was for the Starbucks Card to be perceived as just another gratuitous come-on from an overzealous stranger.

Malcolm Gladwell's "Blink"

Well, coincidentally I recently finished reading "Blink" (the latest book by Malcolm Gladwell, author of the landmark bestseller, "The Tipping Point"), which is all about making choices based on instinct, "in the blink of an eye." At some point in the book, Gladwell even goes so far as to suggest that job interviews would be conducted differently if people were to rely more on their gut feelings.

Writing to my audience about "Blink" would be as much of interest to them as helpful to me in getting my message across.

Now all I had to worry about was the execution. As much fun as I wanted to have with this campaign, I still wanted to keep it simple, and printing the following message on a Starbucks napkin (as though I had written it — impromptu — over a cup of coffee) helped me achieve both of these objectives...

If you've read Blink, the latest book by Malcolm Gladwell (author of The Tipping Point), you know that some of the best decisions are made in an instant — in the blink of an eye. I hope this is one of them. I hope you decide — without hesitation — to sit down with me for a cup of coffee. I would like to show you my portfolio and talk about how I might be able to contribute to the success of Company Name as a creative director, copywriter, blogger and strategic marketing consultant. Please — take your instincts seriously and let's get together soon. Thanks.

Tucked inside the napkin were both the Starbucks Card and a small piece of card stock featuring this short excerpt from "Blink"...

"There are lots of books that tackle broad themes, that analyze the world from great remove. This is not one of them. Blink is concerned with the very smallest components of our everyday lives — the content and origin of those instantaneous impressions and conclusions that spontaneously arise whenever we meet a new person or confront a complex situation or have to make a decision under conditions of stress. When it comes to the task of understanding ourselves and our world, I think we pay too much attention to those grand themes and too little to the particulars of those fleeting moments. But what would happen if we took our instincts seriously? What if we stopped scanning the horizon with our binoculars and began instead examining our own decision making and behavior through the most powerful of microscopes? I think that would change the way wars are fought, the kinds of products we see on our shelves, the kinds of movies that get made, the way police officers are trained, the way couples are counseled, the way job interviews are conducted, and on and on. And if we were to combine all those little changes, we would end up with a different and better world. I believe — and I hope that by the end of this book you will believe it as well — that the task of making sense of ourselves and our behavior requires that we acknowledge there can be as much value in the blink of an eye as in months of rational analysis."*

*Excerpted from "Blink: The Power of Thinking Without Thinking" (pp. 16-17), by Malcolm Gladwell (Little, Brown and Company) [4]

Needless to say, I couldn't help but highlight in yellow the line about job interviews — this was no time for subtlety.

All of the above — the paper napkin, the Starbucks Card and the book excerpt — were mailed in a handsome, cream white A-7 (7" X 5-1/4") envelope that I bought over the counter at The Paper Store. And on the envelope itself, not only did I print the word B-L-I-N-K in big, block letters, but I also added a ring-like, dried coffee stain, introducing the two creative concepts that were the foundation of a campaign that will hopefully land me a new job as a creative director, copywriter, blogger and strategic marketing consultant.

A NEW MARKETING COMMENTATOR WINS NEDMA GOLD

I've been blogging for more than two years now, and I can't say there haven't been days when I've wondered if all the time and energy I put into A New Marketing Commentator is worth it.

But last Thursday wasn't one of them.

That was when the 25th Annual New England Direct Marketing Association's Awards for Creative Excellence were handed out, and this blog was honored with gold.

Yes, this labor of love of mine was the first blog ever to win a NEDMA award, and that award just happened to be first place in one of the Interactive categories (Other Interactive, B-to-B: CD-ROMs, Videos, Interactive Kiosks, Blogs).

How cool is that?

Not to toot my own horn, but I was also fortunate to receive three awards for the direct mail campaign I conducted last year when I ran the Boston Marathon for Children's Hospital Boston. For that initiative, I took home a silver award in the Best Copywriting category, a gold in one DM on a Shoestring category (Budget under $2,500, Consumer or B-to-B) and a bronze in another (Cheap for a Good Cause, Non-Profit).

Of course, it felt great to be on the receiving end of such flattering accolades. I can only hope to find myself in the same beautiful place next year — but not simply as a sole practitioner, as just one member of a whole new team.

[1] Kimmel, Lawrence M. "DM Views: Reflections on the DMA Convention." *DM News.* November 7, 2005. https://www.dmnews.com/dm-views-reflections-on-the-dma-convention/

[2] Blank, Christine. *DM News.* December 5, 2005.

[3] Noyes, Jesse. "Getting in Your Face, Desktop Marketing Takes Off." *Boston Herald.* January 2, 2006.

[4] Gladwell, Malcolm. *Blink: The Power of Thinking Without Thining.* Little, Brown and Company. 2007.

This picture, I believe, was taken as I was leaving the office as advertising manager at Job 3 — an iconic company that sold popular sheet music and song books — in Secaucus, New Jersey, for the last time in 1985.

I'm not working in this picture, but I am in a place where I went to work for a while in 1985-1986. I'm in Iowa, where I went to work at Job 4 in Des Moines. While there, I wrote a lot of direct mail for magazines — Better Homes and Gardens, Country Home, Successful Farming, etc. This was the big leagues for a budding, young copywriter, helping to promote the circulation of a small handful of blue-chip magazines. While the job didn't work out in the long run, the memories will last forever. I met some great people there, and the wide-open spaces were beautiful.

I've been working in the marketing industry for a very long time, many of those years as a copywriter for direct mail and print ads, catalogs and collateral. Check out that big honking electric typewriter in front of me at Job 4. That's how we did it back in the day. Look at that calendar. 1986. Yikes. Long time ago.

This picture of me was taken circa 1986-1987 (I can't quite make out the date on the calendar) when I was working at Job 5 in Franklin. This was a great job at a great direct mail fundraising agency. I wrote direct mail for a roster of exemplary nonprofit organizations including Project Bread, The Jimmy Fund, the Italian Home for Children and The New England Home for Little Wanderers, just to name a few.

In 1990, I joined Toastmasters, a world-renowned organization that helps members improve their communication, public speaking and leadership skills. Toastmasters gave me everything I needed to make presenting in front of an audience a big part of my career.

Take me to your leader.

Or maybe you *are* the leader. Whichever the case, I'd like to talk to the leading decision-maker at your place of employment. The individual who might be interested in what Cargill Creative has to offer.

Who is Cargill Creative? Me. Bob Cargill. Your neighbor here at Edgewater Hills ██████. I am a freelance advertising copywriter specializing in direct mail. I write everything from brochures and letters to catalogs, inserts and space ads. My clients include magazines, book publishers, non-profit organizations, high-tech firms, advertising agencies and many other companies just like yours.

Before opening up Cargill Creative last spring, I held copywriting positions at some of the direct marketing industry's most highly-regarded companies, including RCA Direct Marketing, Meredith Corporation, L.W. Robbins Associates and Jordan-Savage Direct.

My intention this spring, however, is to expand my own client base. And with a little help from friends like you, I think I can do it in relatively short order.

What's in it for you? For starters, I'll give you a crisp, new one-dollar bill just for calling ██████ and giving me a lead. I'll bring your money right over after talking to you. Promise. And if your lead should turn into a job, you'll earn a lot more than a buck. You'll get 10% of my fee. That's right, a full 10%! For instance, if I sell a $1,000.00 job, you'll get $100.00. Not bad for a simple phone call, eh?

Of course, I don't expect you to recommend Cargill Creative without knowing anything about me nor having seen my copywriting. So when you do call, I'll give you a list of my references. And, along with your one-dollar reward, you'll also receive several examples of my work to keep and examine.

So go ahead. Make a call. And get a buck. Take me to your leader today.

Call Cargill Creative at ██████ now.

In 1990, I left a very good full-time job a direct response marketing agency to start my own business as a freelance copywriter. To drum up some new business, I wrote, printed and distributed this flyer to the doors of all my neighbors in a very large apartment building. I'm guessing there were well over 100, maybe even two hundred or so. I was asking them to introduce me to the leading decision-maker at their place of employment. I offered them a $1 bill for the introduction and 10% of the deal if there was one. Entrepreneurial, wasn't I?

124

direct talk

BY ELAINE TYSON

Bells, Whistles *and* Substance

Step into my parlor...Kick off your shoes and pour a tall, cold one. There. Now we can take a leisurely, appreciative look at a direct mail package that combines strong basics *and* some pizzazz...

This *Science News* package takes full advantage of lots of known response-enhancers. But it's much more than just a collection of gimmicks. It goes far beyond being merely technically correct. It has real style, as well as copy that's as appealing as it is informative.

The package is rather expensive—about $315 per thousand, according to Donald Harless, vice

to be barcoded for postal discounts. The envelope's teaser copy is quite intriguing enough to lure prospects inside: "Children who know cigarettes as well as Mickey Mouse...Whales so hungry they take a bite out of the beach...Grasshoppers so smart they change coats to beat the heat...and other things that will make you go 'Hmmm...' Revealed Inside!" And a cut-out allows the "FREE" sticker on the order card to show through.

president/business manager, Harless reports that the promotion, designed by Cargill Creative, has been the control for three years now, although new creative is tested every six months.

The promotion is oversized to stand out in the mail, but not too large

Inside, there's an 11" × 17" folded four-page letter, a 22" × 11" four-color brochure, a nifty lift letter and an order card bearing the sticker.

The letter's copy tone is commendably personal and friendly. This is a good example of long copy that begs to be read. It clearly states the

benefits of *Science News:* "You stir your imagination and add to your intellect. You learn about significant things that are happening in every area of science. Exciting things that are making the world a better place in which to live. Things that will satisfy your thirst for knowledge. Things that will make your life easier on the job, in the classroom, in the lab, or at home." And every benefit claim is backed up with specific examples from editorial.

The lift letter, which begins, "I liked the magazine so much I became the publisher...," reinforces the sale by providing a personal, believable story from the publisher and still more reasons to subscribe. [For more on lift letters, see June '95's Direct Talk.]

The order card makes the most of the extremely strong 12-issues-free offer (which works out to three months of this weekly). The headline says it all: "Not One, Not Two, but...12 Issues Can Be Yours WITHOUT SPENDING A CENT." There's also a clearly-stated guarantee, a motivational respond-by date, and the sticker involvement device, with instructions for using it. (One concern: It does seem odd that the outer envelope, although showing the "Free" sticker, doesn't mention that *12 issues* are free...)

But all in all, there's an admirable feeling of continuity throughout this package's creative work. It makes the most of available bells and whistles, but uses them to enhance, rather than substitute for, the basics that are the foundation of every successful direct mail package. **cm**

Elaine Tyson is president of Tyson Associates, a Ridgefield, CT-based direct response agency and circulation consulting firm.

A very positive review of a direct mail package I wrote for Science News back in the early '90s, perhaps the most successful project of my career so far.

When I had my own business, Cargill Creative, for seven years in the '90s, I conducted a lot of self-promotional campaigns. For one of them, I sent 50 1/2 pound bags of coffee to prospective clients to generate leads. Not only was it an effective initiative, it won the Best of Show award at the New England Direct Marketing Association Shoestring Awards show in 1994.

Smelling the Coffee

What better way could there be for an agency to illustrate its creative direct mail capabilities than by sending out an imaginative direct mail package?

That was the motivation behind Framingham,

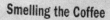

MA-based Cargill Creative's recent two-step mail campaign aimed at drumming up new business for the small firm.

The effort kicked off with 50 postcards mailed to magazine circulation directors and managers across the country with the headline: "Have I Got a Scoop for You!" Each card was handwritten by the president of the agency, Bob Cargill.

Without 'spilling the beans," Cargill alerted recipients to watch their mailboxes for a special free gift, compliments of Cargill Creative. The postcard also featured information on Cargill's expertise in direct response creative.

One week later, the prospects received a box. Inside they discovered a half-pound of gourmet coffee in a resealable pouch with a label that read: "If

> **A memorable package plus a bold offer: the result, a strong brew**

you haven't hired Cargill Creative, wake up and smell the coffee."

Underneath was the agency's address, along with its phone and fax numbers.

The package also included a three-page letter, a reply card and return envelope. The letter began: "Some opportunities aren't meant for the back burner. This is one of them...." It

went on to describe Cargill's experience, the awards given the agency and the like.

But there was also a bold offer: "Give me an assignment. I'll give you my very best work. And if you don't like what you see, I'll redo it until it meets with your approval. That's right, we're talking unlimited revisions — at no extra charge."

That's an offer any prospect would have a hard time refusing.

The coffee metaphor worked well not only editorially, but practically as well: who wouldn't love a package of freshly ground Mocha Java to brew up each morning at work? It's too early to gauge response to this effort, but the agency expects it to perk up first-quarter business. **D**

COPYWRITER: Bob Cargill
ART DIRECTOR: Bob Cargill

An article written about a self-promotional campaign I conducted for my own business, Cargill Creative, which won Best of Show at the New England Direct Marketing Shoestring Awards in 1994.

The 10 Qualities of the Professional Freelancer

Here are ten good qualities a freelance copywriter or graphic designer need to succeed as a professional. If you are a freelancer, have fantasized about such an existence, or simply hire these sole practitioners, the following list is for you.

1. **Fastidious.** A freelancer has to be excessively critical of his or her own work and take great care to do everything right, because there is no one else to blame but yourself if something goes wrong.

2. **Resourceful.** A freelancer must be able to deal skillfully with new problems and unique challenges, because each job is going to be different and each client expects you to be -- or, at least, *become* -- an expert in their field.

3. **Enthusiastic.** A freelancer should approach his or her craft with spirit and intensity; that way, you will enjoy your work days and the bane of your existence, deadlines, won't be so intimidating.

4. **Experienced.** A freelancer should possess a body of work and a history in the business for two reasons: 1) You need to show *prospects* what you have done in order for them to become *clients* and; 2) You need to *know* the rules before you can *break* the rules.

5. **Lionhearted.** A freelancer needs to be extremely courageous in order to succeed. To run your own business takes guts. You are out there on your own. You have to be willing to take risks. And able to take the heat when the pressure is applied.

6. **Artistic.** A freelancer must express his or her creativity. You have to be able to look at things differently, do things differently, and dare to be different yourself. As Pablo Picasso once said, "Some painters transform the sun into a yellow spot, while others transform a yellow spot into the sun."

7. **Nocturnal.** A freelancer should be prepared to work long hours, often well into the night, in order to complete his or her assignments on time. There are moments during the day -- meetings, phone calls, etc. -- when it becomes obvious that the only block of uninterrupted time you are going to come by is when the day is over.

8. **Congenial.** A freelancer needs to know how to win friends and influence people. Be agreeable and positive in nature and disposition. Clients will like doing business with you and networking will come easy.

9. **Educated.** A freelancer must know a lot about a lot of things in order to work successfully with a variety of clients. Read voraciously -- books, magazines, newspapers, the Internet, you name it. Attend seminars. Ask questions of your mentors and peers. And never close your mind.

10. **Rebellious.** A freelancer needs to question the norm in order to find a better way of doing things. You are a hired gun. Someone who has stepped out of line and been called on to run with the ball. Don't be a troublemaker. But don't be a conformist, either.

This was a manifesto, if you will, that I wrote In 1995 about the 10 qualities of the professional free-lancer using the letters spelling out F-R-E-E-L-A-N-C-E-R. For instance, "Fastidious. A freelancer has to be excessively critical of his or her own work and take great care to do everything right, because there is no one else to blame but yourself if something goes wrong."

FRAMINGHAM'S
'junk mail' king

NEWS PHOTO BY KEN McDAGH

Bob Cargill loves to create the mail we hate to get

By Robert F. Dixon
BUSINESS EDITOR

NATICK — To most of us, it's junk mail.

But for many businesses, it's cash flow, the very lifeblood of their existence. About 70 area business people gathered at the Crowne Plaza this week to hear industry expert Robert Cargill unravel the mysteries of successful direct mail campaigns. The seminar was sponsored by the MetroWest Chamber of Commerce's Small Business Council.

Your mailbox is stuffed with all those

Eight years ago, he started his own company. It was tough at first, he recalls, but today he's involved in "about a dozen projects a month" and has done direct mail campaigns for everyone from local retailers like Bernardi's to national organizations like the Mutual Fund Investor's Association and *Atlantic Monthly*.

Just last week, Cargill received a "Shoestring Award" from the New England Direct Mail Association for a low-budget promotion he did for the Dana-Farber Marathon Challenge. The Franklin man designed a mailer he sent to friends and business associates, asking them to sponsor him in the cancer center's annual fundraising run. He raised $1,800 for Dana-Farber Cancer Institute.

Cargill defines direct mail as advertising or promotional material designed to

I don't know if being called a junk mail king is a good thing or not, but either way I sure was proud of this headline back in the day (circa 1996).

Michael Granoff and I did quite a bit of work together back in the day.

A clever postcard promoting one of my presentations as a free gift. How could I not have such a big smile on my face?

My office, which was a large open cubicle, at Job 8.

The New England Direct Marketing Association (NEDMA) has always been very good to me. I have been a member of this group of New England marketing professionals since 1990 and have made a ton of friends thanks to all of our volunteer activities and business networking together. I was president of NEDMA in 1999-2000 and was named its Direct Marketer of the Year in 2009. That was the biggest honor of my career so far. I've also won over 40 NEDMA awards for my work over the years. I'm currently a proud member of the board of directors there. Oh, and then there was the time I got to walk out on stage at one of NEDMA's big gala events back in the day wearing a fancy, formal tuxedo and escorted by a Marilyn Monroe lookalike model/impersonator. Good times. Great memories.

A little peek inside my office at Job 13. You can see some books, awards and pictures, but not my desk and the nice window view I had of the outdoors.

PLease heLP ouR dad
heLP Kids who aRe'NT
as LUCKY as US!
SCOTT,6 aNd BEN,3

Bob Cargill and his
two sons, Scott and
Ben, during The Boston
Marathon in 2002

Help two Sudbury kids and their dad help The Home for Little Wanderers.

To help Scott, Ben and their dad help The Home, mail your check (payable to The Home for Little Wanderers) to Bob's attention at 33 Oakwood Avenue in Sudbury or go to www.thehometeam.kintera.org, where you can donate online. Thank you.

Dear Friend,

For many of us, childhood was a fairy tale, and our grownup years are following suit. But for some kids out there, life isn't all good.

That's why I'm running The Boston Marathon in 2003 for The Home for Little Wanderers. This nationally renowned, private, nonprofit child and family service agency ensures the healthy development of children at risk so that they, too, can know what it feels like to be lucky and loved.

Please "sponsor" my marathon run and give as much as you possibly can -- today. I'll appreciate it. The Home will appreciate it. And, most of all, the kids there will appreciate it. On their behalf, I can't thank you enough."

Bob Cargill
33 Oakwood Avenue
Sudbury, MA 01776
978-443-4022

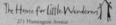

The Home for Little Wanderers
271 Huntington Avenue
Boston, Massachusetts 02115
1-888-HOME321
www.thehome.org

I was happy and honored to be able to run the Boston Marathon not once, but twice for a client of ours at Job 13, The Home for Little Wanderers.

I took this picture recently from the road between The Innovation and Design Building and the Flynn Cruiseport Boston. Imagine, my office when I worked at Job 14 was in one of those overhangs between buildings. Coolest office ever.

Here's a look inside my office at Job 15, yet another nice work environment. Spacious. Comfortable. Quiet. Perfect.

I have been a member of the New England Direct Marketing Association since 1990. Beth Drysdale (middle) and Pat Lee (right), who I have always enjoyed working with, have been the association's managing directors for almost that long.

I remember Michael Chinnici as the first designer I ever worked with at my first job as a copywriter in 1983. He is someone I have always looked up to with admiration and respect as both a professional and friend. I am so happy we have been able to stay in touch after all these years. This picture of us was taken not too long ago when we met up to reminisce over a cup of coffee at Starbuck's in Framingham, Massachusetts.

Receiving the Direct Marketer of the Year award from the New England Direct Marketing Association in 2009 was the greatest honor of my career so far. Here I am proudly holding the award, which I still prominently display on the desk in my home office, with Gary Lubarsky and Alex MacAaron.

From where I sat during Job 19 in 2016, everything was looking up. Great job. Great office. Great colleagues. Great boss.

Working with Pam Sullivan was always a pleasure. Our paths have crossed many times over the course of our respective careers, including here at a conference in New Hampshire not too long ago.

I was fortunate to serve as president of the American Marketing Association's Boston chapter for fiscal years 2018-2020. Here I am with Meghan McGrath, who succeeded me as president of the chapter for fiscal year 2020-2021. Photo by Jonathan Sachs

I have been a member of the New England Direct Marketing Association since 1990 and the president of the association in fiscal year 1999-2000. I have also been fortunate to have received over 40 awards from them including this one in 2019 for my series of videos about social media I had shared on LinkedIn.

I'm not a painter, but I'm much more of an artist than a businessman. At least that's how I've felt about myself all these years. My inner creativity has always been begging to come out amid my career in the corporate world.

LESSON 16 DEVELOP LEADER- SHIP SKILLS

LESSON 16
DEVELOP LEADERSHIP SKILLS
IF YOU WANT TO MAKE YOURSELF INDISPENSABLE, MAKE YOURSELF A LEADER. BRING OUT THE BEST IN OTHERS. DARE TO TAKE INITIATIVE. INSPIRE THOSE AROUND YOU TO THE POINT WHERE YOU'VE BUILT YOUR OWN COMMUNITY, PEOPLE WHO HAVE YOUR BACK BECAUSE THEY KNOW YOU HAVE THEIRS.

2006-2008

There I went back to the attic, my own little garret, a respite from the cold, cruel world, shelter from the storm. Only I didn't want to make a habit of spending too much time in this room. While it was my home office, working from home wasn't quite so common then as it is now, so it didn't necessarily mean things were going your way.

They certainly weren't going my way.

I found a few projects to work on, a freelance job here, a small writing gig there, but nothing to keep me too busy for long.

Fortunately, I was saved by Judy. The first time I remember speaking to her on the phone was at the end of yet another long work day as a contractor that left me feeling like I was doomed to a failed, boring career.

Talk about a pivot. She was calling about a truly exciting role with a big, growing company in Lexington, Massachusetts that was disrupting the space in which they did business. They were all about e-commerce, direct marketing, printed products and technology. I was soon to be their new senior copywriter.

While the title was a downgrade, the role, responsibilities and place where I would be working were certainly a step up. I wasn't going to be the creative director, or even the associate creative director (which I had been used to being ever since I had my own business), but the work would be similar.

I was going to be working on the client side, too, similar to the first three jobs of my career. My mission would be to hire and manage a team of copywriters who would be writing emails, banner ads, landing pages, pop-ups, direct mail, postcards, and anything else you can name to help promote sales of this company's goods and services.

There were so many things I loved about this position.

The writing was right in my wheelhouse. Most of the assignments were short, quick and to the point.

This company knew how to move fast, too. I liked the accelerated pace. There was never a dull moment. Almost every day, I started and finished at least one project, sometimes more. That's how many projects I alone got done there. Countless. Multiply that times the number of writers on my team as we grew, and you'll have a sense of our high level of productivity.

We were crushing it.

Everything was so methodical — how teams were organized, how meetings were run, how performance reviews were given and how new hires were interviewed, you name it. They left no stone unturned at this company, and I've never worked for another one like it.

This company was a well-oiled machine, to put it mildly.

What I didn't like was that I had to sit in a cubicle here, which was a relatively rare situation for me to have found myself in during my career. I felt exposed, conspicuous and vulnerable, like a fish in a bowl without a place for privacy.

I got used to it, though.

What I wasn't able to get used to was a persistent, painful physical health problem that surfaced early in my tenure there that necessitated a minor surgical procedure. It wasn't anything serious, but for some reason it took a humongous emotional toll on me. Even now I want to keep what it was a private matter, but it triggered a depression in me that I've been struggling with most of my adult life. I went through an incredibly difficult midlife crisis during this time, where I was as low as I've ever found myself. Fortunately, I fought through this mental health crisis tooth and nail, and came out of it successfully.

There were so many highlights of my time working at Job 16. This is where I really cut my teeth writing emails, as well as banner and display ads.

While I was there, we had some kind of program that made it possible for customers to order something akin to fast-food advertising and marketing services. I managed a small team of copywriters who worked on these projects. They were writing pieces of work in hours versus what might have ordinarily have been days. Kudos and props to the company's powers-to-be at the time for this brilliant idea, even though it required incredibly industrious creative people to pull it off. That they did, and congratulations to all those involved in this initiative.

In my entire life, I've only been out of the country twice. One of these times was thanks to this ridiculously awesome employer. They sent me to Barcelona, Spain, for a week.

Surprisingly to others, though, at first I didn't want to go. My obsessive-compulsive disorder was getting in the way. It makes traveling far away, especially alone, difficult for me. I actually enjoy an adventure. I'm generally not afraid to take risks. But for some reason, my OCD kicks in big-time whenever I am not around familiar territory. I can't explain it. So, naturally I was very worried about leaving the country, not to mention that I was going to be away from my wife and children for such a long time.

But I eventually made the trip — it was my responsibility to go, after all — and it was the best business trip of my life so far. I felt I played an instrumental role in our team meetings there. I was quite proud of myself.

What an experience, overall, especially the night I was trying to order food all alone in a small restaurant and the language barrier was clearly getting in the way. That was a comedy of errors on my part if ever there was one. Except for the few years of French I took back in the day, I am the furthest from being bi-lingual. I was out of my element, clearly.

I need to get away more often, I know.

Back home at the office, this company had an amazingly good way of celebrating the end of the work week. Every Friday night, they provided employees with free food and cold beverages at 5 p.m. as their way of bringing everybody together to reward them for their hard work. What a great idea! However, sometimes I would have so much work on my plate that I would just go downstairs to grab a drink and a few appetizers and bring them back to my desk so I could continue working. But other times, yes, I would find myself staying late not to work, but to hang out with my colleagues.

What was not to like?

This may have been the first job where I started listening to music on something other than an old-fashioned radio while I worked, as this seemed to be a thing among my colleagues. A lot of them had earbuds and iPods.

It wasn't unusual for me to have to knock on somebody's desk to get their attention when I wanted to talk to them, as they usually had their head buried in their computer screen and whatever they were listening to turned up loudly. It may have been annoying at first, but I eventually got used to it and, as I said, I later picked up the same habit, only being the older guy among the team, I'm guessing the volume of what I was listening to was much lower than those around me.

While some of my colleagues may have already been on Facebook (if they were relatively fresh out of school), it was during this time in 2006 that this social media network opened its doors to not just college students, but to everybody else. I was already on LinkedIn, of course (as I have already mentioned, I was one of the first million to join this online networking platform out of the over 800 million members today), and my blog had been up for a while now, but this was a big milestone in social media history. I signed up shortly after permission was granted to adults, and I was enamored with it from the get-go.

Where had Facebook been all our lives? How had we survived before it? This was a game-changer on so many levels for so many people, both personally and professionally, certainly for yours truly.

While the company didn't have a public, consumer-facing blog, we did have an internal blog which was available to employees only. I contributed to it quite frequently, even putting my own blog on pause for a while.

Twitter was founded while I was working at this company, too. I was starting to get a big hankering for working in the social media field, which seemed like it would be super exciting and incredibly varied as opposed to the same old repetitiveness of what I was doing at the time.

There was an incredibly rigorous interview process at this company. I had to go through the paces myself, of course, when I got my job there. Now it was my turn to ask the questions. Each job candidate was interviewed by a team, each member of the team coming from a specific and distinctive perspective. So when all was said and done, we had a 360-degree view of the candidate that helped ensure the right hires were made.

I relished the opportunity to be a leader at this company. I felt like a big fish in a big pond. Not all the time, but often enough to keep me fulfilled. Ultimately, that fulfillment wasn't enough, but for a very good period of time, relatively speaking, my job satisfaction was high.

I had been tapped to speak about our department to new employees during their orientation period. It felt especially good to be perceived as a company veteran and an industry expert. It was also a great way to get to know your fellow employees before they had even settled into their new digs.

I was also managing a large team, about 20 staffers or so at one point. This was after I had been there a couple years. While I started out managing only writers and helping to build that team, I was now managing two teams of designers, both the retention and acquisition teams.

That meant a lot of weekly meetings with the respective groups, as well as one-on-ones with them individually. Oh man, if those walls could talk. Some of those meetings were like group therapy sessions, others more like halftime huddles during the big game, with me playing the coach giving the big, rousing pep talk.

Those weren't the only meetings I was attending, either. I was constantly being invited to meetings via Outlook, invariably without being given the option to opt out. My attendance was required in so many meetings that I was having difficulty finding the time to complete my deliverables, the copywriting and creative direction for which I was responsible.

I really liked my one-on-one meetings with my boss, though. We had some great conversations. She was not just my supervisor, she was the consummate teammate and one of my biggest supporters. I will always be a fan of hers. She would say that she had my back, words that I really appreciated, words that I share with others often today, thinking of her inspiration, encouragement, optimism and leadership.

"I got your back." Who doesn't like to hear that from their boss? Thanks, Loraine.

Overall, I took my responsibilities very seriously, doing my best to be a positive, influential role model to a host of predominantly younger marketing professionals, knowing I could be making a difference between their success and failure on the job.

I forget what the exact occasion was, but I remember giving a talk about Seth Godin's book, *Purple Cow*, to a large group of colleagues in my department, many of whom reported to me. My intent was to inspire and motivate those around me by introducing them to someone I knew to be an icon. Seth Godin was, and still is, a big influence on my career. He's someone I look up to, admire and respect for his marketing prescience.

During that presentation, I gave away a copy of *Purple Cow* to someone in the audience. That person reached out to me not too long ago on Facebook, years after that occasion, saying how much that meant to him, that he still has the book and he was inspired by that gesture. That meant so much to me.

One of my last presentations on the job here was to a group from my department with whom I spoke and took the opportunity to share the movie, *The Last Lecture*, which was delivered by Randy Pausch, a professor in computer science at

Carnegie Mellon University in Pittsburgh, Pennsylvania, shortly before he passed away from cancer.

He had written a very moving book (which went on to become a bestseller), and this was the video of the last lecture itself, which he gave to his class shortly before he died. In this lecture, Randy encouraged his students to seize the moment and make the most of every day they are alive.

That's how I have always felt about my own life, including my career, which is one reason why I may have moved so quickly from job to job over the years. I've never wanted to stay stagnant, never wanted to grow tired of a routine. I have always wanted to be challenged and feel like I am making the most of myself and the opportunities that come my way, because you never know when your time is going to come up.

For some reason, I taught myself early on in my adult life that it is important to go for it, not to wait for it, and that is how I live both my personal and professional lives to this day.

I didn't want to leave my job there, but I couldn't resist the opportunity to join another company where I had been offered a job as a creative director. It was stubborn and short-sighted of me, in retrospect, but I was determined to have that title again, even if it meant leaving a good job too soon to get it.

I was managing quite a large team of well over a dozen copywriters and designers. The salary was good. The bonuses, and benefits, too. I even had stock options.

But I was after that title, not to mention the chance to focus more on social media. I was after that fame.

Plus, I would be getting an office, not sitting in a cube, which is something that, well, didn't sit well with me, as superficial as that might sound to others.

My impatience got the best of me yet again. It was a bittersweet time. On the one hand, I couldn't wait to get back to agency work with the job title I felt I deserved and doing work I believed I would enjoy more. On the other hand, I couldn't help but think twice about everything I was going to be leaving behind: colleagues who respected me, a very successful company with a very bright future, a fantastic boss, work I had grown accustomed to, not to mention that generous salary.

Like almost everywhere else I have worked during my career, I was caught between a rock and a hard place.

I didn't stay much longer. I left for what I thought would be a more suitable professional place for me. I left to go to work at what we will be calling Job 17 in this book.

LESSON 17

COMMUNICATION SKILLS ARE INVALUABLE

LESSON 17
COMMUNICATION SKILLS ARE INVALUABLE
COMMUNICATING EFFECTIVELY IS A KEY TO SUCCESS. MOST SENIOR-LEVEL EXECUTIVES ARE THOSE WHO CAN COMMAND AN AUDIENCE IN WORDS, EITHER WRITTEN OR SPOKEN. THE DEVELOPMENT OF STRONG SKILLS IN WRITING AND PUBLIC SPEAKING WILL CARRY YOU FAR.

When I tell people I have a diverse professional background, I'm not exaggerating.

Working at a large e-commerce company was a rare client-side experience for me, as most of my career I have worked in agencies. My clients at the previous job were internal, people within the building tasked with different objectives in different channels — acquisition versus retention, direct mail versus email, etc.

In the agency world, our clients are external. Companies, businesses and brands hire us to serve as their agents, if you will, helping them to promote sales of their products and services.

"Do you want to go back to being a creative director?"

Words to that effect in an otherwise short and simple email from Alan, the owner of a local digital marketing agency, while I was still working at another job caught my attention. I soon had an interview with him and an offer I couldn't refuse. The job title certainly appealed to me. But there were many other things about the job that were attractive. I wanted to do more social media, which he was promising me. I was anxious to get back to the agency side of things. And the thought of going back to a small, entrepreneurial shop as opposed to working in a big corporate environment appealed to me.

I was in.

Like other job moves of mine in the past, I made the switch with mixed feelings, wondering what I was getting into and worrying about how much I was leaving behind.

Nothing ventured, nothing gained, though. So, off I was on a new path, this time around working more as a consultant, strategist and social media practitioner, doing some copywriting and some public speaking. A nice variety of responsibilities, overall.

A company meeting at this agency included around as many employees as a team meeting at my previous job. There were around 15 of us in an office space about the size of the lobby of the building where I worked previously.

The pace and pressure were different from what I had grown accustomed to at the e-commerce company. I was working my tail off, as always, but there were fewer projects in the queue here than there. It was easier to manage.

The work was completely different. It was digital marketing, sure, but it was for a diverse array of clients. It was agency life as I had known it.

While I had put my own blog on hold and wrote for the internal company blog during my time working at Job 16, here we had our own public blog that I began posting to immediately. This meant the world to me. I have always been a writer by trade, someone who loves sharing words with as many readers as possible. This was a treat.

Alan gave me complete freedom in this department, the autonomy I craved. I look back with gratitude for the faith Alan placed in me. I wrote a boatload of blog posts about marketing and social media here, many of which garnered quite a bit of attention from the outside world. This was my sweet spot.

I also handled most of the agency's social media while I was there, not to mention our clients'. That was my primary focus.

I would have weekly calls with each of these clients, explaining our social media activity on their behalf as well as the results. We would talk about things like how many tweets we shared, how many retweets we got, how many comments we received, how many clicks through to their website our work resulted in and how many leads as a result.

While my previous job was the beginning of my education in digital analytics, this job was my deeper dive into this area of importance. As right-brained as I had been up to this point in my career, I was now being challenged to use my left brain almost as much.

My specialty has always been the creative side of things, but when it comes to digital marketing — as opposed to traditional marketing — especially in the modern marketing era, every professional in this industry is expected to work with both sides of his or her brain.

Reporting became part of what I did, whereas in the past the writing and creating was all I had to worry about.

Indeed, technology has made what I do for a living more powerful and effective, yet more challenging and frustrating as well. Anyone in marketing today who has been around for a while can attest to how much the industry has changed, and how one-trick ponies are now dinosaurs.

You can't rest on your laurels. You can't be a specialist. You've got to be a master of all trades and a jack of none.

Today, in fact, a lot of the work I do in social media requires me to provide data and analytics as well. This was never ever the case back in the day. I merely provided the creative, the copy and the design. Often just the copy.

Speaking of copy, I wasn't only doing social media here. I was also getting some great opportunities to write landing pages, email and copy for websites. It was a nice mix. As an agency, we were very strong at lead generation and digital marketing, but we were also a force to be reckoned with when it came to creative.

The highlight during this time of my career was a very pleasant surprise. I told you about my involvement in the New England Direct Marketing Association. I joined the New England Direct Marketing Association in 1990 and have been an active member ever since that time. I was president of the association in 1999-2000 and have won over 40 awards from them for my copywriting and creative direction.

But I had never won this particular award.

Out of the blue one day, I found myself on the phone with a New England Direct Marketing Association board member, who was informing me that I had been selected as their Direct Marketer of the Year. Wait! What? Me? To say I was beside myself would be an understatement. I was elated. This was akin to a lifetime achievement award, in my opinion, and I didn't think I had achieved nearly as much in my career at that point as I had hoped to when all was said and done.

But this was big news to me nevertheless. Huge news. I was at once honored and humbled, thinking of the others who had received this award in the past. Big names in my book. Professionals at the top of their game in of the marketing field in New England.

My colleague, Aaron, wrote a very nice blog post about my receiving the award. And the agency presented me with a ridiculously awesome congratulatory cake and office party, which was extremely kind and thoughtful of them.

I was feeling down at the time, struggling with my self-esteem, so this special honor and my employer's recognition meant a lot to me. It was a saving grace, personally.

Yes, winning the New England Direct Marketing Association's Direct Marketer of the Year award in 2009 was a welcome shot in the arm, as I wasn't feeling good about myself at this time in my career. I was thinking about how much I was vacillating in my goals. I felt like I was drifting rather than steering, and I needed to regain control of my direction if at all possible.

I eventually suggested to Alan that I reduce the hours that I was working there at the agency, and he kindly agreed to that arrangement. We worked out a deal where I would be there on a part-time basis only, with the balance of my time spent serving my own clients.

What I especially liked about Alan as a boss was he was always very calm and reassuring. He spoke in a gentle, soft tone of voice that put others at ease. To this day, I appreciate the confidence he had in me and the opportunity he gave me.

While at my previous job, I used to meet at Panera Bread for meetings with clients and friends about social media — like my own very tiny side gig — now I was meeting all over the place with different people who were inquiring about how to use Twitter, Facebook, Instagram and the like.

We're talking about social media 101, which to this day is still something most executives haven't mastered — the basic how-to's, principles and practices — what many businesses, companies and organizations still aren't teaching their employees, what many schools still aren't teaching their students. Yet this has become a necessary skill set among the workforce, certainly if you are in marketing, advertising, PR, publishing or any kind of corporate communications.

I really enjoyed the next year of my part-time employment working at Job 17, but my bank account certainly took a hit. While I managed to bring in a number of projects on my own, it was not nearly enough to equal what I had been earning as a full-time employee, including benefits.

What I loved most about working there was how much social media I was able to do not just for clients, but also for ourselves as an agency. I loved writing my blog posts. I enjoyed teaching clients how to use social media for business. I had fun teaming up with Alan — who was super smart and a pleasure to work with — to deliver webinars and live, in-person presentations. The emails and landing pages I wrote there reflected best practices and looked awesome, too, as our design staff was top-notch. I felt good about all the work I had done there.

Where was my next stop and how did I find it? Like a cat has nine lives, I'm fortunate to have had many good breaks. I've had my share of failures, losses and even beatdowns, but I've certainly risen more times than I've fallen, even if I've had to count on someone else to help me get back on my feet.

All blog posts in this chapter, Chapter 17, were written by Bob Cargill for the Nowspeed blog and are republished here with permission.

O O O

OLD-SCHOOL MARKETING PRINCIPLES IN A NEW-MEDIA WORLD

If your job has anything to do with marketing, not much has seemed to go your way lately. Not only has a slumping economy been working against you, but thanks to Google, social media networking, the Internet and an overall explosion of new media, today's consumers and business prospects have never been savvier and more in charge.

As marketing guru Seth Godin wrote in his book, Meatball Sundae...

"Consumers have more choices than ever before. More media choices, more choices or products and services. There aren't three TV networks; instead, there are a million (literally) things to watch on YouTube. There aren't a dozen radio stations; there are a million (literally) online. As a result, the consumer has the power to say, "If I'm not interested in what you have to say, I won't watch it. I'm not a hostage any longer." [1]

Given such rampant intolerance among your target audience to practically anything resembling a sales pitch, you certainly have your work cut out for you. But that's where today's so-called new marketing strategies can help, each and every one of them going a long way toward enhancing the efficacy of your more tradition-al, outbound marketing initiatives, including email, direct mail, print, etc.

For starters, you and your organization should already have launched a blog in order to engage in the kind of open, candid conversation with your constituents that will, ultimately, earn you more of their loyalty, trust and support. If you haven't established a presence in the blogosphere yet, that is one big step you really ought to consider taking post haste.

In addition to blogging, there are countless other social me-dia-related activities — using such tools as Twitter, LinkedIn and Facebook, just to name three — that would certainly be beneficial to your organization and its constituencies. Before embarking on your own SMM initiatives, take time to read social media maestro Chris Brogan's primer, "If I Started Today," which will lay the groundwork for your first few steps onto the SMM playing field. Advergirl's recent four-part "Social Manifesto — How Companies Are Using Social Media" includes some excellent information and insight, too.

But all that advice doesn't mean you can't succeed in marketing today the old-fashioned way. Quite the contrary. There are still plenty of opportunities for purists, traditionalists and even the raw neophytes among us to leverage the timeless, tried-and-true principles of our trade.

A Classic Mail-Order Ad

Take Cushman's Fruit Company, for example. Demonstrating the right way to harness a few proven, age-old direct response advertising strategies, Cushman's was selling 24 of its legendary HoneyBells in a quintessential, full-page mail-order ad that ap-peared in the November 23 edition of PARADE Magazine.

Just how classic was this ad? First of all, the written words alone had incredible stopping power, beginning with a headline in the form of a curious question...

"What the devil is this?"

Then Ed bit into one and the plot thickened....

Following the headline above was an extraordinarily interesting, cleverly written story about Ed Cushman and the origin "of the strangest looking, fiery-orange, bell-shaped oranges anyone had ever seen."

In addition to such original, copywriting craftsmanship, what really helped this ad stand out was its compelling positioning of HoneyBells as "available once and only once each year."

A little like, well, tickets to a Red Sox-Yankees game or a Barack Obama Inauguration Medallion from The Bradford Exchange, HoneyBells do not come around often. They are, in effect, a limited edition...

"This is your first, only and last call for Cushman's 2009 crop of legendary HoneyBells," the ad reads, substituting an orange icon in the shape of the fruit for its actual name. "They'll be hand-picked, packed and shipped to lucky recipients in just a few weeks. After that, there are no more. Anywhere. At any price. So, you must order now. Or wait until 2010."

Talk about leveraging the law of supply and demand.

And as if that's not an irresistible enough offer, every shipment of HoneyBells includes "free HoneyBell bibs (juice protection), HoneyBell tattoos, a lighthearted HoneyBell story (a rib tickler) and directions on HoneyBell feasting (an art)."

Sweet!

And, naturally, Cushman's includes a guarantee of satisfaction, which as any old-school direct marketer knows, is always a great way to optimize response rates.

Old Marketing + New Media = Successful Marketing

The lesson to be learned here is that in this day and age, not every marketing communications initiative has to be built online — there is still a place and a time for the traditional mail-order ad. But just as important: the new marketers who are doing their thing in a post-Cluetrain Manifesto world have as much to leverage from old companies like Cushman's as Cushman's does from us.

I'm thinking that a good formula for successful marketing today is to combine old-school, proven marketing principles with all the new marketing tools, technologies and strategies you can deploy.

Think about it: what could Cushman's do with a blog? And what could you do with an ad written like Cushman's'?

THE SIX FEARS OF FACEBOOK AND OTHER SOCIAL MEDIA CHANNELS

Given my entrepreneurial, extroverted and — some might say — experimental personality, it's only natural that I started blogging in 2004 and have enthusiastically embraced Facebook, LinkedIn and Twitter, to name just three of the many social media communications channels and tools that are so wildly popular today.

I enjoy the free exchange of information, knowledge and opinions. And I've never been shy about opening myself up to others.

Yes, like a kid in a candy store, I'm enamored with the Internet, giddy and practically overcome by the extraordinary power it gives me to make new friends and business contacts so easily and quickly.

I admit it. I can't get enough of it, this life in a post-Cluetrain Manifesto world. To me, it's intoxicating and addictive. It's fun, not work.

But despite my passion and partiality for building community — and striking up new relationships — online, I realize there are still many detractors and holdouts, those who would rather shake hands and swap business cards than trade tweets, pokes and links. Some may be technologically challenged. But most seem to be uncomfortable with the notion of complete and utter transparency, stuck on the same, old questions about what to say in such a public forum and how others will react to their communication streams.

I understand.

After all, no one wants to embarrass themselves — or worse, jeopardize their career over something they said.

And besides, those who have not yet jumped on the social media bandwagon are right on at least one account. No online tool will allow for the intimacy and authenticity of face-to-face conversation.

But I still think the pros of using social media far outweigh the cons. And so does my wife, Barbara. Yes, even though she wondered aloud for months why literally millions of users — including her husband — were so smitten with Facebook (we're talking over 150 million active users, in fact, according to this January 7 announcement by founder and CEO, Mark Zuckerberg, on the Facebook blog), she's now singing this social utility's praises for having connected her with dozens of friends and opening up a whole, new world of communications with them.

The truth is that the reason Barbara hesitated to take the plunge and sign up for Facebook until just a few weeks ago is pretty much the same one that others — especially business people and corporations — are taking so much time to dip their collective toes in the social media waters in general.

Fear.

That's what I learned from my wife about Facebook and social media...and that's what I would like to share with you here. Most people hesitate to join the online conversation for fear of the following...

The Six Fears of Facebook and Other Social Media Channels

1. Fear of the Unknown. *It's only human nature to be afraid of the unfamiliar, to cling to routine and status quo. Barbara knew about the popularity of Facebook for a long time. But the mere thought of it was daunting to her. It was overwhelmingly new and different, a strange, distant world. And that's the same feeling I sense among many of my colleagues, peers and clients. It's fear bordering on paralysis.*

"Sure there are success stories among the big companies that have dipped their toes in the social-media water," writes blogger and social media strategy consultant, B.L. Ochman, in this recent AdAge article. "But the vast majority of giant companies are still absolutely terrified of social media."

Yet everyone I know who has joined the social web, feels remarkably at home there, comforted by the fact that they are surrounded by like-minded friends who understand what it means to reveal some of this and share some of that, building trust, goodwill and a warm, fuzzy feeling that we are indeed all in this together. The outcome of all of this activity is new and improved relationships that we might not have had otherwise. And not just with former classmates and old flames, either — with valuable, new contacts, leads, business prospects and clients, too.

2. Fear of the Loss of Privacy. *I can't tell you how many times I hear others cite confidentiality issues or just plain shyness as their reasons for not adopting social media. On the one hand,*

I'm deferential to those who prefer discretion to transparency, independence to community. But I also think any fear of going public on the social media circuit is unwarranted and misguided. In many cases, you are the gatekeeper to information you post about yourself or your business. As Barbara quickly learned, you don't have to connect with someone you don't know or anyone you don't like. And you don't have to share anything that is, in fact, privileged information.

But perhaps more important to note is just how many others — young and old alike, working professionals and homebodies (all of whom might be classified as members of Gartner's Generation V, by the way) — have already jumped on the social media bandwagon. Who wants to be left behind?

3. Fear of Having Nothing to Say. *Like me, Barbara always has a lot on her mind. But for some reason she was concerned she'd have nothing to say on Facebook. That's preposterous, I told her, knowing that her free spirit, sense of humor, interest in popular culture and knowledge of current events would play well in a virtual community. And it has. She just had to wait until she was ready to put herself out there.*

As it was for my wife, that's how it is for many business folks, too. They may have tons of experience, expertise and news about everyday endeavors to share with others. Not to mention all that good personal information about themselves that uncovers the emotionally endearing, refreshingly human side of business. Yet many still hem and haw over taking that first big step.

In a recent post on his blog, Chris Koch (who writes about B2B marketing in the technology industry) said...

"Indeed, the only thing scarier for marketers than being responsible for a corporate blog where people can say anything they want about you and your brand is the prospect

161

of having to sustain it — to keep coming up with smart, thoughtful things to say. Forever."

4. Fear of Rejection. *The bigger the organization, the bigger the fear of negativity and criticism, of naysayers and competitors taking shots at the brand. Barbara had such trepidation concerning her own personal brand identity before joining Facebook. What if she was called out for saying something silly? What if none of her friends connected with her? But just as Sally Field once exclaimed on stage, my wife was soon shouting, "you like me, you really like me!"*

Sure, the stakes are much greater when stock prices, sales and jobs are on the line. So not everyone — or more to the point, every conversation — is suitable for social media. Obviously. But what most constituents find after a short time spent immersed in these new online communities is that the atmosphere is invariably civil and chummy, almost quid pro quo-like. As long as you're truthful and trustworthy.

5. Fear of the Time Commitment. *Yes, it takes time to write a good blog, to share a link on Facebook, or to answer a few questions in a LinkedIn group. Sorry. There is no automatic pilot in social media. Like any worthwhile endeavor, you get out of it what you put into it. But that doesn't mean you have to give your life over to it. Few of us can be as active, prolific and visible in this space as the likes of Chris Brogan, David Meerman Scott, Guy Kawasaki and Joseph Jaffe. But like any good relationship, if you're going to be social, you do need to touch base regularly. Barbara, for instance, checks Facebook for a few minutes several times a day — to connect with close friends, to post comments, ask questions, update her status, etc. That's all, though. Slow and steady may not win the race, but it will put you in the middle of the pack. And from a strategic point of view, that's not necessarily a bad place to be, given how new this is to most participants.*

6. Fear of Failure. *Have you ever played in a golf tournament? If so, then you know what it feels like to tee it up in front of a gallery, all eyes on your attempt to drive the ball long, straight and clean. Like speaking in public or, yes, hitting a golf ball in front of a watchful crowd, contributing original content online — coupled with the thought of, yikes, baring one's personality — strikes fear in the hearts of even the most intrepid professionals. After all, we're talking history here. What happens on the Internet, stays on the Internet. So obviously, no one wants to risk looking bad. But that's just the point: Human beings, by nature, are imperfect and flawed. So theoretically, we shouldn't be afraid to adhere to perhaps the most important principle of the social web, which is to keep it real, always.*

In a recent guest post ("Generation Y in the Workplace Explained") on Chris Brogan's blog, Teresa Wu wrote...

"While Generation X continues to emphasize the importance of maintaining a professional online image, we who grew up using Facebook and MySpace as places to share our photos and lives with our friends don't want to turn it into a purely professional arena. I've found that the most meaningful connections I've made were when I've exposed the more personal aspects of my life."

So remember, it's not just okay to be transparent and authentic, open and honest on Facebook, LinkedIn, Twitter and wherever else you may be on the social web, it's imperative. Take a lesson from Teresa Wu. Or from my wife, Barbara. To face the six fears of Facebook and other social media channels, just be yourself.

◼ ARE YOU A CORPORATE ALL-STAR?

Whether it's delivering an outstanding presentation at an important trade show, winning over a client with an awesome display of creative firepower or simply going above and beyond on everything that's asked of you, there are many obvious ways to score points with your boss. But now you can add blogging, tweeting and even spending company time on Facebook to that list.

It's true. Workers who use social media — even if it's for their own personal branding — can go a long way toward positioning their employers as thought-leading organizations worthy of their constituents' trust, loyalty, support and business.

That's what I'm telling you today. And that's what I told the 40 or so people in attendance at my recent social media marketing workshop for the New England Direct Marketing Association. Citing Edelman Digital's recently released white paper, "Five Digital Trends to Watch for 2009," I was happy to proclaim that thanks to social media, everyone in the audience had the opportunity to be so-called corporate all-stars (if they weren't already)...

"Personal branding, while not a new concept, is hot. Many workers are flocking to social media venues in an effort to invest in their own brands, especially in these more uncertain times. Smart companies are recognizing that these individuals, if channeled, can become corporate all-stars that help them market in a very efficient and authentic way," reads the summary of this Edelman Digital white paper.

Ironically, I found out about this white paper on Micro Persuasion, a wildly popular blog written by a quintessential example of the corporate all-star, Edelman's own Steve Rubel. If you're not paying attention to Micro Persuasion, you're missing out on arguably today's most vital information and insight on "how

164

emerging technologies are revolutionizing marketing communications." Trust me. I've been reading Steve's posts since I started blogging myself in 2004, and I find him to be engaging, illuminating and downright spot on almost every time in his analysis and commentary.

Other well-known corporate all-stars active in social media circles on behalf of their employers include Chris Brogan, Sarah Evans, Jeff Brooks, Kara Swisher, Amber Naslund, Frank Eliason and Paul Chaney, just to name a small handful of the many who are undoubtedly out there tirelessly, indefatigably working the beat.

As Seth Godin writes on page 35 of his latest book, Tribes, "The essential lesson is that every day it gets easier to tighten the relationship you have with people who choose to follow you."

And that's due in large part to the emergence of social media, of course. If you're blogging, tweeting and engaging in the conversation on Facebook and other SM platforms, you're likely positioning yourself as a leader of a tribe, someone who values listening and learning as much as teaching, someone who can be counted on as a successful brand ambassador, corporate citizen and role model. The benefits to you and your employer are multitudinous, including...

• Increased credibility and enhanced reputation

• Greater transparency, authenticity and trust

• More knowledge, information and insight

• Additional PR and business opportunities

• New relationships, contacts, customers and friends

• Extra traffic, attention and buzz

• Greater professional growth and education

So what about you? Are you a corporate all-star? Are you doing everything you can to hit a home run out of the social media ballpark? If not, there's never been a better time to step up to the plate.

FIVE IMPORTANT QUESTIONS TO ASK YOURSELF BEFORE YOU USE SOCIAL MEDIA

In preparation for the Social Media Marketing 101 seminar I'm leading for the New England Direct Marketing Association on March 3, I've been giving considerable thought to not just the mechanics of social media, but also to the guiding principles that apply to using this new form of online communications effectively. After all, so many are so intrigued — if not enamored — with simply the notion of joining the conversation. Yet far too few are fully aware of the long-term, strategic rules of engagement on the social web.

Indeed, social media should not be looked at as a fast track or shortcut to a successful exchange of information. When leveraged appropriately, this vast array of online tools, utilities, platforms and channels can lead to deep, mutually-beneficial relationships between people and organizations. But it is not a panacea or quick fix for an inability to find common ground with your constituency in the first place.

Those who are most successful with social media are comfortable in their own skin, willing to reveal their personalities and unhesitant to share. They are thought leaders and inveterate readers, people who value listening and learning as much as teaching others about their own respective areas of expertise. Their social media activity is really just an extension — better yet, an encapsulation — of who they are already. It is their online pro-

file, their individual brand identity, an aggregation of everything they are as human beings and professionals.

Those who are most successful with social media include men and women such as Chris Brogan, Todd Defren, Ann Handley, Joseph Jaffe, Kel Kelly, B.L. Ochman and Steve Rubel, just to name a handful of role models and rock stars among this space.

So before you decide to dip your toes in social media, take a few minutes to answer the following five questions. If you can answer yes to at least a few of them, then you're in a pretty good place, a position from which you can at least begin to immerse yourself in such relatively uncharted waters as the blogosphere, the Twitterverse, Facebook and the like. If not, then you need to move the needle in these areas and possibly talk to a third party specialist who can provide consultation, support and assistance.

Can you embrace the two principles of social media, authenticity and transparency? If you can't be yourself as a communicator, you can't be a good candidate for social media.

Does your company's culture allow for, if not encourage, entrepreneurialism and innovation? For those who are private, protective and totally buttoned-up, social media represents a radical departure.

Are you comfortable with inclusive, informal dialogue among all levels of employees and between your organization and others, including detractors? Social media levels the playing field for all concerned.

Do you understand that to be successful with blogging and other forms of social media communications, you need to listen, engage and become an active, generous member of the "community" at large? Ask not what social media can do for you, rather what you can do for it.

Are you prepared to devote the time, energy and resources to creating quality, relevant content on an ongoing basis, which will be shared — for the most part, unconditionally — with your friends, followers, clients and possibly even competitors? A commitment to social media is a game-changing move.

10 SURPRISING SIMILARITIES BETWEEN BLOGGING AND DIRECT MARKETING

As a veteran copywriter and creative director, someone who's made a living for over two decades putting together direct mail, email and direct response advertising campaigns that pitch practically every product and service imaginable, I may not fit the mold of the typical blogger.

But I've been helplessly hooked on blogging since my first post in 2004, never able to get enough of this newfangled mode of online communications. I like it for many reasons, first and foremost because it's such a refreshing change of pace from tired, traditional marketing riffs and age-old corporate-speak.

In the blogosphere, the prevailing communications standard is transparency, not verisimilitude. There's no spinning of the truth. And you're only as successful as you are trustworthy. But if you commit your time and energy to it, blogging can be an incredibly effective way to disseminate news, information and opinion to an audience of readers who are predisposed to be interested in what you have to offer.

Sure, blogging is all about being open, honest and yes, vulnerable. Its most ardent devotees believe passionately in sharing generously with their audiences, engaging them frequently in particularly candid conversations in public forums where everyone has an equal voice. So it's not necessarily the first place you'd turn if your priority is, say, e-commerce. But the number of similarities between blogging and direct marketing tell me the two disciplines don't have to be mutually exclusive. Not at all. For instance...

1. Measurable. Of course, many of the benefits of blogging are qualitative, not quantitative. But the fact that search engines such as Google and Yahoo are so quick to pick up blogs, especially when they're updated regularly, is certainly a big plus. And there are many other blog metrics worth measuring, too — including subscribers, visitors, comments, third-party citations, inbound links and more — using tools such as Google Analytics, BlogPulse, Technorati, Icerocket and Clicky, among countless others. You may not be able to gauge the success of a blog in response rates and ROI the way you would measure the results of a direct mail or email campaign. But you shouldn't be using it the same way, either. In establishing their positions as thought leaders and practice experts, the best bloggers among us are building trust and credibility, flushing out leads on behalf of their corresponding brands.

2. Targeted. Like the most strategically designed direct marketing campaigns, most blogs are geared toward an audience of constituents and customers, like-minded people who are most likely to do business with the blogs' authors and sponsors. For three exemplary examples of well-targeted, niche-oriented blogs, check out Yvonne DiVita's Lip-Sticking, Jeff Brooks' Donor Power Blog and Laura Ries' Ries' Pieces. Bloggers need to know who they're writing for, what's going to resonate most with their readers and move them to action.

"Make sure that you are primarily focusing on a particular topic, and the more specialized that topic is, the better you'll do. It's also key to step back and evaluate whether there are enough prospective readers in your chosen niche. It's better to be brutally

169

honest with yourself than to toil away and end up disappointed," writes Copyblogger's Brian Clark in "10 Effective Ways to Get More Blog Subscribers." [2]

3. Offer-oriented. Sure, blogging isn't selling, per se. It's listening, sharing and conversing, primarily. And your offer isn't a product or a service, either. It's your attention to your audience. But like any good relationship, the more you put into it, the more you get out of it. You can't expect an immediate return on your investment in blogging, not before you've established a degree of authority in the blogosphere. But once you've earned a reputation as someone worth following, the likelihood is that your wares will be looked upon more favorably and you'll see an increase in sales. John Jantsch's Duct Tape Marketing is an excellent example of a blog that helps sell its author's products and services, as is Hubspot's Inbound Internet Marketing Blog, which features lead generation offers (webinars, educational kits, etc.) at the close of each post.

4. Interactive. What's always been regarded as one of direct marketing's biggest benefits is, unlike broadcast advertising, the fact that it's a form of reciprocal, two-way communications, giving the sender the ability to trigger a response from the receiver. If your audience responds favorably to your offer, you have a hit on your hands. It's that simple. What could be better? Well, some might say blogging. After all, not only can a blogger get a yes or no answer from his readers, he can also get opinion, feedback, input and advice. While, in many cases, direct marketing is a well-choreographed sales pitch to an audience of passive prospects, one of the attributes of a blog is that it allows readers to provide honest, public comments that are posted below the author's spiel. Blogging involves and engages readers. By granting the opportunity to respond almost instantaneously to any and all posts, a blogger is building a relationship with his or her constituency. As the level of confidence grows between blogger and reader, so does the potential for lucrative, new business activities.

5. Inspirational. *You may already be familiar with the acronym, AIDA. It stands for Attention, Interest, Desire and Action. It's something direct marketers always have in mind when working on a campaign. And it's what every blogger should heed, too. Think about it. Your blog isn't worth anything if it doesn't capture your audience's Attention. You then need to hold their Interest and create a Desire for something, whether it's more sharing of your expertise and opinion in subsequent posts or products and services your organization has to offer. It's at that point that you want your readers to take Action. One way or another, the best bloggers among us — Chris Brogan immediately comes to mind — have a way of inspiring their readers to act on their feelings through support, loyalty, devotion and investment of both time and, ultimately, money.*

6. Personal. *"People respond best to authenticity," writes Susan Hanshaw in her post, Direct Marketers Know More About Social Media Than You Think, on the Inner Architect blog. And I couldn't agree more with her. Having written literally hundreds of direct mail and email letters over the course of my career, I've always gone to great lengths to put myself in the shoes of the actual letter signer, whether he or she was a CEO of some huge corporation, a publisher of a magazine, or an executive director of a nonprofit organization. I had to be him or her. But blogging leaves little room for such impersonation at all. Such stark transparency on the part of those bloggers who "get it" goes a long way toward bridging any existing communications gap, fostering trust, respect, understanding, appreciation and some degree of business activity.*

7. Experimental. *One of the tenets of direct marketing is the testing of one approach against another, the experimentation* with offers and concepts in order to identify those elements of your campaign that resonate with your audience. And once you've found your sweet spot, of course, you don't hesitate to take advantage of it until something better comes along. The same goes for blogging. You can alternate between long posts and short ones and see which ones are more popular. You can test guest bloggers versus your own staff writers. You can count comments on different topics and issues. You can include a variety of outbound links in your posts and watch which ones are clicked through more than the others. You can share news and information about yourself and your organization, your field of expertise or anything else under the sun. And at the end of the day, when all is said and done, the approach you should settle on is the one readers like best.

8. Creative. In direct marketing, the longstanding 40-40-20 rule suggests the success of a campaign is equally dependent on the list and the offer, while its creative execution is worth the remaining 20%. I've always questioned the preciseness of those percentages, but I've never disputed the upshot of the rule, which could just as easily apply to blogging. Your creative should support, not predominate. The look and feel of a blog should be clean and simple, colorful and aesthetically attractive only to the degree that it is reflective of the author's and sponsoring organization's brand identity. A blog needs to stands out among the clutter, sure. After all, there are now well more than 100 million blogs in existence. But for the most part, what a blog should be remembered for is good, relevant, regularly published content, not bells and whistles.

9. Formulaic. While the artist in me has always been hesitant to embrace anything too formulaic, my business instincts are strong enough to pull me toward industry best practices (not without incorporating a measure of creativity to stand out from *the crowd). That's how it is for me as both a direct marketer and blogger, but that's not to say there aren't other ways to approach either discipline. While your blog should be a direct reflection of you and your brand, anyone in the blogosphere should be mindful of the space's established principles and practices, many of which are covered in detail in Naked Conversations, Join the Conversation, The Cluetrain Manifesto and Social Media Marketing: An Hour a Day. In addition to the aforementioned books, read blogs written by the likes of such luminaries as Chris Brogan, Debbie Weil, Seth Godin, Steve Rubel, B.L. Ochman and Beth Harte. Blogging has been around long enough now for a whole cadre of experts and evangelists to have paved the way for your own success.*

10. Powerful. *Yes, like direct marketing has been for so many decades, blogging has quickly established itself as a powerful communications tactic to be strategically leveraged by advertising, marketing, PR and sales professionals.*

"Listen to the murmur of your market," wrote Don Jackson in "2,239 Tested Secrets for Direct Marketing Success," the book he put together with direct marketing guru, Denny Hatch. "Create feedback loops in your database environment so that you can record what your customers and prospects are saying about your products, your service, your company and your competition. There is no more valuable source of information." [3]

If you ask me, a blog is one such "feedback loop," a way of interlocking a circle of people who are interested in you and your organization and establishing a mutually beneficial relationship with each and every one of them.

And if that's not direct marketing, it sure is similar.

THE CURE FOR THE COMMON SOCIAL MEDIA PRACTITIONER

Now that so many organizations — both commercial and non-profit — have begun to at least experiment with social media, if not make a serious commitment to it, standing out among the cacophony of posts, comments, tweets, requests, invitations, updates, podcasts, images and video clips calling for attention is no easy task.

On the one hand, much of the content being leveraged, repurposed and produced originally for dissemination via blogs, Twitter, Facebook and the like is not ready for social media prime time. Yes, unfortunately, too little of it is authentic, transparent and extemporaneous enough. And even if you can overcome that challenge, you still have to contend with the so-called "Attention Crash," the inability of people to deal effectively with the surfeit of information in their lives.

As Steve Rubel, SVP, Director of Insights for Edelman Digital (the digital practice of Edelman, the leading independent global PR firm), wrote on August 28, 2008 on his phenomenally popular blog, Micro Persuasion...

"Though the current global financial crisis grabs all the headlines, there's another storm quietly brewing — a crisis of attention scarcity. The inputs we have into our lives — that which we allow and those that are forced upon us — are exceeding what we are capable of managing."

"The Attention Crash is here and it will only get worse. There will always be more content vying for consideration."

So what's a social media practitioner to do in order to be heard loud and clear above the din of so much online activity, never mind responded to favorably? How do you as a marketer or a PR pro or perhaps even an intern who's been hired to build a con-

stituency of friends, fans and followers command attention and respect for the brand you represent?

Well, take it from a practitioner of another kind, a neighbor of mine who just happens to be a pediatrician, and be mindful of the three A's.

The three A's —Ability, Affability and Availability— are a requirement on his job as a caregiver to young patients and their families, the good doctor told me in a passing conversation we had recently while watching our boys play baseball. And the three A's, in my opinion, should also be required of anyone who hopes to make uncommonly meaningful, mutually beneficial connections in social media...

1. Ability. *Don't underestimate what it takes to be proficient in social media. It doesn't take years of schooling to write what you're doing in 140 characters or less, but it does take more than a modicum of talent to earn the respect and reputation that you need to be successful on Twitter and other social media properties. The fact is that the most acclaimed practitioners in this space are specialists, authorities and knowledge leaders not just online, but in their physical lives as well. They are visionaries who are renowned for their expertise wherever they go, people who are able to articulate their thoughts such that they resonate with, if not inspire, the masses.*

2. Affability. *Skills alone will only get you so far in social media. You need to humanize your brand identity. Those who are most popular in social media are those who have the best "bedside manners," the most engaging personalities. They are amiable and congenial, generous and kind, people who are as good at listening as they are teaching, as humble and humorous as they are confident in their abilities. They are people like Chris Brogan, Paul Chaney, Joseph Jaffe, Steve Rubel, Ann Handley, Beth Harte, Yvonne DiVita, Susan Hanshaw and Sarah Merion, among others.*

175

3. Availability. *Like a physician on call, to be appreciated by your constituents in social media is to be open for business practically 24/7. No, you're not saving lives, but you are demonstrating that you are responsive and attentive to those who want to connect with you. It's one thing to establish a presence in the blogosphere as well as on Twitter, Facebook and LinkedIn. But if you want to be looked up to as the real deal that you are in this space, you have to be on the grid more often than not and be prepared to lose a little sleep.*

HOW TO WEAVE CAUSE-RELATED MARKETING AND FUNDRAISING TACTICS INTO YOUR SOCIAL MEDIA PROGRAM

Now that most brands and businesses have finally dipped their toes into the social media waters and are making themselves heard on Twitter, Facebook and throughout the blogosphere, many of them are wondering what to do next with these relatively new communications platforms.

In fact, besides an obvious — and understandable — fear of social media, that's the main reason so many organizations have hesitated to go in this new direction with their marketing in the first place. Not everyone is sure how to use social media yet. And there's certainly still a lot to learn about measuring and monetizing it.

After all, it's one thing to be tweeting, updating and blogging. It's quite another to be parlaying such activities into actual conversations and transactions of the business variety.

But there is a social media marketing strategy that appears to have caught on out there, one that can help marketers like you do well by doing good for others, one that Minneapolis-based

176

Target Corporation leveraged recently by way of its "Bullseye Gives" campaign (which I've already written about here), in which the retailer asked its audience to go to its Facebook Fan Page and choose — from a list of 10 — the charities it should "give to the most."

The idea is to integrate cause-related marketing and fundraising tactics into your social media program so that your constituency will follow, friend and fan you out of kindness and generosity as much as their interest in your products and services.

If you're supporting a charitable cause, others are more likely to support you in turn — and spread the good word on your behalf.

Wrote Brian Morrissey in Adweek in an article about the "Bullseye Gives" campaign (Adweek, "Cause Marketing Meets Social Media," May 18, 2009)...

"For brands, particularly those in low-consideration categories like consumer goods, charities can become a cheap way to get access to the megaphones everyone has in social media." [4]

To the author's point, I would just add that by joining forces with charities, brands and businesses of all kinds can appeal to the sense of altruism in everyone, providing their constituents with real incentive to act for the sake of giving, not getting, all the while positioning themselves as caring and considerate entities that are truly in touch with the community at large.

As Scott Henderson, Cause Marketing Director for MediaSauce, said in an interview with Beth Kanter on Beth's Blog: How Non-profits Can Use Social Media...

"Consumers want to know that the businesses they patronize are doing something for the greater community, not just for themselves." [5]

So if you're about to take the plunge on your own social media program and you really want to make a splash, don't overlook the power of cause-related marketing and fundraising. The tactics involved are only as limited as your imagination. You could...

Make a donation for every one of your followers, friends and fans.

Reward a re-tweeter with a contribution to his or her favorite charity.

Leverage the popularity of consumer-generated media (CGM) and ask your audience to tell you — in words, pictures and videos — where to put your charitable dollars.

Post frequently about a cause or nonprofit organization you believe in strongly.

Stage a contest among a short list of charities, with the one making the best case for the furtherance of its mission receiving a substantial donation from you.

Give away your products or services in the form of a free "makeover" to those who are less fortunate than you.

Host a fundraising event that brings together like-minded people on behalf of a good cause.

Encourage your constituents to develop their own unique ways of giving back to the community, lending your financial support to those who demonstrate the most initiative, innovation and inspiration.

Indeed, there are many ways to call attention to your social media activities so that your efforts on Twitter, Facebook, blogs and the like aren't in vain. But giving a piece of the action to your favorite nonprofit organization may be the best of them all.

According to Gavin O'Malley in Online Media Daily (Online Media Daily, "Conventional Cause Marketing Evolves Via Social Media," March 15, 2009)...

"In the United States, IPG's Lab found that 92% of consumers said they have a more positive image of a product or company

*when it supports a cause, while 87% said—when price and qual-
ity are equal—they are more likely to choose a brand associated
with a cause." [6]*

*The bottom line is if you're wondering what to do next with social
media, try giving support to a charitable cause. What you'll get
in return may be a pleasant surprise.*

MEET ME AT THE INTERSECTION OF SOCIAL MEDIA AND MARKETING

*While I've always believed in the principles and power of direct
marketing, as soon as I started blogging in early 2004, I realized I had discovered something that could very well have a huge
impact on the future of the industry in which I earned my livelihood.*

*I'm no prognosticator, but I saw for myself what the authors of
The Cluetrain Manifesto had written in their groundbreaking
book, that, among other things, "markets are conversations" and
that "there are no secrets. The networked market knows more
than companies do about their own products. And whether the
news is good or bad, they tell everyone" and that "companies that
don't realize their markets are now networked person-to-person,
getting smarter as a result and deeply joined in conversation are
missing their best opportunity."*

*I didn't want to miss that opportunity. I didn't want my employers
and clients to miss that opportunity. And I didn't want the direct
marketing industry to miss that opportunity.*

*So while for so many years I had espoused the beliefs and heeded
the advice of such direct marketing legends as Bob Stone, Lester
Wunderman, Joan Throckmorton, Herschell Gordon Lewis and
Denny Hatch, now I was reading books and blogs written by*

new marketing gurus and social media pioneers like Seth Godin, Joseph Jaffe, Robert Scoble, Yvonne DiVita, David Meerman Scott, Steve Rubel and B.L. Ochman — and hanging on every word.

And not only did I become a blogging aficionado, I became a blogging evangelist, preaching to anyone and everyone who would listen about what I thought were the benefits of this new-fangled, self-publishing platform.

While I was once solely focused on the list and the offer and the benefits and a guarantee and getting a good response, now I was thinking about authenticity and transparency and immediacy — but yes, still getting a good response.

While I was once believed that companies had the upper hand in their communications with consumers, I was rapidly beginning to realize that online communities (or "markets," as proclaimed in The Cluetrain Manifesto) had the real control and that marketers had better join the conversation — and listen to their constituents — or forever hold their peace.

But I never once thought direct marketing and blogging had to be mutually exclusive...not at all.

In fact, on April 9, 2004, in my blog (this blog), I wrote...

"...isn't true direct marketing all about initiating a one-to-one dialogue with a mass audience (oxymoronic concept aside)? "Listen to the murmur of your market." That's what Don Jackson writes on page 116 of "2,239 Tested Secrets for Direct Marketing Success," the book he put together with Denny Hatch in 1998. He tells readers: "Create feedback loops in your database environment so that you can record what your customers and prospects are saying about your products, your service, your company and your competition. There is no more valuable source of information." [7] Exactly. This blog is one such "feedback loop." It's one way of interlocking the circle of people who visit us through our Web site — and establishing mutually beneficial relationships with each and every one of them."

That was then. This is now.

Now we have studies like Michael Stelzner's, sponsored by the Social Media Success Summit 2009, saying that (according to this article at Marketing Charts)...

"An overwhelming majority (88%) of marketers in a recent survey say they are now using some form of social media to market their business, though 72% of those using it say they have only been at it a few months or less."

Now I find myself using not just blogs, but Twitter, LinkedIn and Facebook as much as direct mail, email and other non-social media on behalf of my clients.

Now I don't feel so alone among my peers in the direct marketing community when it comes to talking about — and actually using — social media.

Indeed, like Bob Dylan once sung, "the times they are a-changing" — fast. And it is my belief that those of us direct marketing, advertising and PR professionals who can leverage social media technologies and tools to build long-lasting, mutually-beneficial relationships with colleagues, clients, customers, connections, friends and fans will be much more successful amidst this new communications era.

What about you? What do you believe? Where do you stand at the intersection of social media and marketing? On one side or the other or smack dab in the middle with me?

Note: Earlier this year, I was honored and humbled to be named the "Direct Marketer of the Year" for 2009 by the New England Direct Marketing Association (NEDMA). This post is an adaptation of the speech I had the opportunity to give to an audience of my peers upon acceptance of the award on May 6, 2009 during NEDMA's Annual Conference at the LaCava Center at Bentley University in Waltham, MA.

10 WAYS TO SUCCEED IN SOCIAL MEDIA BY BOB CARGILL

This 2,700-word post was initially published as a series of individual posts on Bob Cargill's blog, A New Marketing Commentator, between January 13-April 5, 2010.

Now that so many businesses are using blogs, Twitter, Facebook, YouTube and other social media channels to connect with their constituents, it's only a matter of time before they realize what a challenge it is to use them successfully. No, social media isn't rocket science. But it's definitely a BIG departure for those who have been dependent on traditional marketing, advertising, PR and corporate communications methods up until now. So to help educate and enlighten those who are about to use this relatively new means of engagement for the first time, here's a list of 10 ways to succeed in social media...

1. Adopt the right company culture.

I hate to disappoint you, but not every organization is cut out for social media. To those who are accustomed to privacy and top-down, one-way, interruptive communications, it requires nothing short of a transformative change from the inside out.

The truth is that those who are most successful on the grid are more than willing to share their institutional knowledge, comfortable in their own corporate skins and not afraid to reveal their personalities. They have no secrets. They have no fears. They're open and transparent, genuine and authentic, honest almost to a fault.

Yes, businesses that get social media have no problem whatsoever with inclusive, informal dialogue. They encourage entrepreneurialism, welcome competition and frown upon micro-management. They know that to succeed in social media means to worry a lot less about control and much more about support and empowerment of their friends, fans and followers.

2. Set realistic expectations.

Using social media to communicate with others isn't that difficult. But if you expect your posts, tweets, status updates and videos to result in any new leads or business opportunities, you had better be more than a little patient and perseverant.

As I've written before (The Importance of Getting Past the Social Media "Dip")...

...social media shouldn't ever be looked at as a fast track or short cut to success. Mastering social media requires a long-term, strategic investment that needs to be looked at as part and parcel of almost everything else you do as an organization, not as a quick fix or panacea for an inability to find common ground with your constituency in the first place.

Don't disappoint yourself. Be realistic with your expectations. To put together an effective social media program, you need to be as prolific as you are informed, as personable as you are inspirational, capable of producing a stream of original content on a steady, uninterrupted basis that your constituents will find not just interesting, but worth their valuable time.

The fact is that the most successful practitioners in this space are specialists, authorities and knowledge leaders, people who are renowned for their expertise wherever they go.

Are you one of those people? Does your organization have folks like that at its disposal? If so, then you have every reason to believe that your social media efforts will bear fruit.

3. Create enough quality content.

One of the most common mistakes I see people and businesses make in social media is jumping into it without having anywhere near enough original, quality content to stay in it for the long haul. Either they underestimate just how critical it is to be able to offer news, information and opinion for an indefinite period of time or they simply don't care about being fully engaged.

Whatever the case, these folks invariably run short of content and ultimately have no idea what to say anymore. So relationships are interrupted. Momentum is lost. And their constituents are left wondering why the "brand" they look up to is suddenly so silent in social media.

But it doesn't have to be that way.

Before dipping your toes in the social media waters, it behooves you to have an arsenal of content ready and waiting for launch. But you also need to be prepared to create and share (sometimes on the fly) an endless stream of new content — blog posts, human interest stories, opinion pieces, instructional videos, status updates, etc. — via such social media channels as Twitter, Facebook, LinkedIn and the like.

Social media is a labor of love, an inexhaustible work in progress, something you do day in and day out, not only when it's convenient for you.

Social media is not a commitment to be taken lightly. It's a serious, long-term obligation you have to your friends, fans and followers — both your internal and external stakeholders — from the get-go. So don't go into it prematurely.

4. Stand for your brand.

As much as you need to be yourself in social media, it's even more important to be a positive, well-suited reflection of the organization you represent.

So before you blog, tweet or record that YouTube video, take pause and ask yourself if you're actually capable of embodying the very best characteristics associated with your brand. Even if you're your own boss, you may find it more than just a little challenging to come across as a trustworthy, authoritative and engaging spokesperson.

The truth is that some of the most successful social media practitioners are those with extraordinarily good people skills. They're evangelists, diplomats and envoys, folks who live and breathe the topics and issues bandied about among their respective business circles. Their strong sense of corporate identify is eclipsed only by their personal character and integrity. In the best interests of their constituents as much as their employers and clients, they say what they mean and mean what they say. They're natural brand ambassadors.

Does that describe you or anyone on your payroll?

5. Work as a team.

While most social media programs have a single champion at the helm, the best among them have a crew to provide support.

Never mind the extraordinary demands of the job on almost a 24/7/365 basis. From project management to PR, customer service to marketing, creative to analytics, there are simply too many different skills required for one person alone to be successful on the grid on behalf of a big brand.

As I've written before (Social Media is a Team Sport, Not a Solo Act)...

An exceptional writer with a strong body of knowledge, a charismatic personality and a boatload of enthusiasm can make a huge social splash — don't get me wrong. But to sustain an effective strategy for an indefinite period of time requires the input and output of a collaborative, cross-functional group, a small team of people with complementary skills who can tag-team the initiative.

If you're faced with budget constraints or a shortage of talent, that's one thing. But if you're serious about social media, you're going to want a handful of professionals working the beat — strategizing, scheduling, listening, responding, creating, engaging, measuring, you name it. One way or another, you're going to want to work as a team.

6. Leverage a number of channels.

It's one thing to tweet a few times a week, write a blog post once a month and update your profile on LinkedIn if you happen to land a new job. But it's quite another to be active on a handful of social media channels on a daily basis.

That's right, the most accomplished social media mavens don't occasionally go online. They practically live online.

Instead of checking email and voice mail, they're responding to a steady, endless stream of comments, questions and requests from their friends, fans and followers.

Instead of sitting in meetings all day, they're sitting in front of a variety of screens, tap, tap, tapping away in the name of meaningful engagement with their constituencies.

Instead of working nine to five, they're on call morning, noon and night, whenever they're near their Blackberries, iPhones, laptops and notebooks.

But it's not just a matter of putting in all this time. To succeed in social media means to be active in more places than one.

Are you writing a new blog post at least once a week? Are you using Facebook for both personal and professional reasons? On LinkedIn, are you writing recommendations of others, sharing your presentations and participating in groups? Are you logging on to Twitter at least several times a day? Do you have your own YouTube channel? How about FriendFeed, Delicious, Google Reader and Buzz?

Sure, for a number of reasons — time and talent, chief among them — not every social media channel is for everyone. But let's face it, if you're only using one or two of them, you're barely scratching the surface.

7. Overcome the social media "dip."

A common mistake made by many business folks is to think that social media will be an instant cure for what ails their traditional marketing activities. And while in many cases it can and will have an overwhelmingly positive effect on an organization's ability to connect with its constituency, it's not a panacea for an inferior product, poor PR, inept communications or a lackluster brand.

The truth is that it's a long and winding road to social media success. And as anyone who's been blogging, tweeting and the like for a long time knows, it's often an uphill climb, too.

But if you can tough it out — listening, creating, engaging and opening up to others — for an indefinite period of time, making sure that social media is part and parcel of everything you do in business, not a silo, then the odds are pretty good that you'll be a hit on the grid.

As I've written before (The Importance of Getting Past the Social Media "Dip")...

If you ask me, the key to being successful with social media is patience, perseverance and pushing past the so-called "Dip," a difficult stretch of time (invariably the beginning) when the going can be tough and the rewards may appear few.

The Dip, of course, is the title of one of Seth Godin's many best-selling books. On the front flap of the book, the "Dip" is referred to as "a temporary setback that you will overcome if you keep pushing." [8]

But the definition of the "Dip" I like best is written on page 17 of the book, where Seth describes it as "the long slog between starting and mastery." My experience tells me that that's just the juncture, too, where almost everyone involved in social media gets caught up in the "Dip," where people — and brands — have to decide for themselves whether their seemingly Herculean efforts are worth it.

8. Educate others more than you promote yourself.

A big mistake many organizations make is to use social media the way they use traditional marketing vehicles such as direct mail, email, print and broadcast. Instead of listening to their constituents, they're tooting their own horns and focusing on ROI. They're doing everything they can to force one-way, top-down, interruptive marketing messages into channels that were built for permission-based dialogue that doesn't necessarily conform to a preconceived agenda.

What they're doing is like trying to place a square peg into a round hole. Their efforts are futile.

But that's not to say you can't generate leads and sales in social media. In fact, if you conduct yourself appropriately in these spaces and places, chances are your efforts will result in a multitude of new business opportunities.

Use the blogosphere, Facebook, Twitter, LinkedIn and other such properties to share not only your knowledge and expertise, but also a little about who you are as a person and a lot about the industry in which you earn your livelihood.

Create as much valuable content as possible and then give it away for free.

Become a publishing machine, a brand that's much more informative, supportive and educational than promotional.

Put the good word out about your products and services, but do so because you want to help others, not because you're in it for a buck.

In social media, the more you open up to others as a fellow human being, the more they'll get to know you as someone they can confide in, look up to and trust. The more they'll want to do business with you and your organization.

9. Measure the results of your activities.

If you're serious about using social media, not just in it for fun, then you need to measure the results of your online activities so you know where you stand.

If you publish a blog, you can use such tools as Technorati to see how it compares to others in your industry or Google Analytics to find out which posts people are reading, where they're coming from and how long they're staying on your site.

But that's not all you want to analyze. You also want to look at how many readers are subscribing to your blog, how many comments you're receiving, how many other blogs are linking back to yours and how often it's turning up in search engine results.

And that's just for starters. Ideally, a blog should lead to a multitude of new business opportunities — including speaking engagements, PR, WOM, leads and sales — all of which you want to monitor, qualify and quantify.

On Twitter, of course, it's great to have a lot of followers, but how many of them are retweeting you or actually engaging with you? Are you being included on a lot of lists? Are you using bit.ly or another URL shortening tool to track the number of people who actually click through your links? Have others featured you in their Follow Friday tweets?

Among the many tools you can use to assess your performance on Twitter are Twitter Grader, TweetLevel, TweetStats, Twit-Graph and TweetMeme.

Facebook, of course, provides some interesting demographic information to page owners about their fans, not to mention data such as number of "likes," "wall posts," "comments" and "visits." You also want to observe — and respond to — what fans write on your page; that's an obvious way to manage and monitor your brand's reputation.

It's easy to count your connections — or members of any groups you manage — on LinkedIn as well as how many times they interact with you.

And on YouTube, you can track how many times your videos have been viewed, how many subscribers you have to your channel, friends, ratings, comments and more.

And that's just scratching the surface. There's an infinite number of metrics you can monitor in social media, both quantitative and qualitative, all of which you should look at carefully if you want to succeed. And there are many good social media monitoring tools — such as Radian6, Trackur, Cision and Scout Labs just to name four — you can use to do the job for you.

10. Don't take yourself too seriously.

Your success in social media may be dependent in large measure on what you have to share with others, but how you come across — your online persona — is also very important.

Whether you're on Facebook or YouTube, tweeting or blogging, you need to be as affable as you are knowledgeable, as charismatic as you are smart. You need to lighten up.

Sure, many of the most effective social media practitioners are opinionated and authoritative, natural born leaders at the top of their fields. But if you take a closer look, you'll find that they're also *easygoing and deferential, not afraid to share some of their personal lives with their professional peers. They're approachable and responsive, people who are comfortable having impromptu, informal conversations with a diverse range of constituents.*

As I've said before (Blog Post on Video: The Three A's of Social Media Branding)...

Skills alone will only get you so far in social media. You need to humanize your brand identity. Those who are most popular in social media are those who have the best bedside manners, the most engaging personalities. They are amiable and congenial, generous and kind, people who are as good at listening as they are teaching, as humble and humorous as they are confident in their abilities.

Yes, when all is said and done, social media won't work very well for the aloof or the arrogant, those who play their hands close to the vest and can't crack a smile. Social media works best for those who take their work, not themselves, seriously.

10 WAYS TO SUCCEED AS A COPYWRITER

This 2,800-word post was initially published as a series of individual posts on Bob Cargill's blog, A New Marketing Commentator, between July 13-October 31, 2010.

My first job out of graduate school many years ago was as a copywriter for RCA Direct Marketing in New York City. And the rest, as they say, has been history. Since that first exciting stint writing about the most popular records (yes, vinyl) and tapes (yes, cassettes and eight-tracks) of the day, I've written about an incalculable number of different products and services. As I wrote in the preceding post here on A New Marketing Commentator...

I've written copy to help promote everything from business cards to books, healthcare to software, insurance coverage to investment advice, magazines to music, travel to tuxedos and much, much more.

I've also written direct response fundraising copy for dozens of charitable organizations (which, by the way, has been some of the most satisfying work I've done over the course of my career so far).

I may have worked for a number of different companies, developed new skills and taken on new responsibilities — such as creative direction, public speaking and social media — along the way, but I've also stayed true to my roots as a copywriter.

And after all of these years writing headlines and subject lines, direct mail packages and email blasts, blog posts and brochures, teasers and tweets, I've been able to draw a handful of conclusions about what it takes to succeed as a copywriter.

So with all of that said, here's the first in a series of "10 ways to succeed as a copywriter"...

1. Dare to be different.

To earn a living as a copywriter, you have to be a good writer. That goes without saying. But what's almost just as important to your success is your ability to think creatively.

Copywriting is not for the conformists and traditionalists among us. It's a job for those who are willing to take chances and who understand what Pablo Picasso (1881-1973) meant when he said, "Some painters transform the sun into a yellow spot; others transform a yellow spot into the sun."

To stand out among the clutter and competition, your work has to reflect a high degree of originality and inventiveness. It can't be the same old, same old. It has to be new or improved, first time, every time.

Copywriting is for the right-brained and open-minded, those who aren't afraid of being judged for their idiosyncrasies and foibles. It's for those who like to read such books as Seth Godin's Purple Cow, Spencer Johnson's Who Moved My Cheese? and Roger von Oech's A Kick in the Seat of the Pants. It's for people who like to listen to everything from Lady Antebellum to Lady Gaga. It's for well-rounded people with diverse tastes and interests, people who have no problem whatsoever looking at something from someone else's perspective.

2. Care deeply about results.

While being able to exhibit a high degree of creativity may be important to the success of a copywriter, achieving the highest possible ROI is usually imperative, certainly in direct marketing, the industry in which I earn my livelihood.

My brethren and I work with the understanding that the purpose of most campaigns is to promote sales of a product or service, not the copywriter's ability to turn a clever phrase. It's nice to win awards. But what really counts is winning over your audience, those who are hopefully hanging on your every single word.

Yes, what the most successful copywriters really care about is convincing those on the receiving end of their communications to take action in some way, shape or form such as picking up the phone, filling out a form, clicking on a link or passing the word along to a friend. What they want more than anything are leads, orders, referrals and repeat business.

But that's not to say good creative and great results have to be mutually exclusive. In fact, many times they go hand in hand.

For instance, in the early '90s, I wrote a direct mail package for Science News magazine that featured the following teaser on the outside envelope...

Electricity so powerful it shocks a heart-attack victim back to life...

Whales so hungry they take a bite out of the beach...

Grasshoppers so smart they change coats to beat the heat...

And other things that will make you go "hmmm"...

Including that last line — the name of a well-known hit song by C+C Music Factory as well as an expression that late-night talk show, Arsenio Hall, used in his monologues — on the envelope was a demonstration of creativity that more than paid off. After all, this package brought in literally thousands of subscription orders during the few years it reigned as a control for Science News and was eventually honored by the New England Direct Marketing Association with a first place award.

3. Walk in your readers' shoes.

In Stephen R. Covey's best-selling book, The Seven Habits of Highly Effective People, Habit #5 is "Seek first to understand, then to be understood." [9] Well, that's also one of the habits of highly effective copywriters. They seek first to understand everything they possibly can about their audience before they even begin to attempt to be understood themselves.

Yes, the more you know about your customers and constituents, the easier it is to make a potentially valuable connection with them.

Unfortunately, that's much easier said than done.

Tight schedules and small budgets often supersede any opportunity to look closely at the demographics — and psychographics — of those whose attention you covet. But that doesn't mean you can't find out what makes them tick.

What you really want is the chance to hear directly from customers, prospects, donors or stakeholders, people who can provide you with credible, honest feedback about your client's products or services. That's where a focus group can be a big help (if it's an option).

There are plenty of other ways to research your audience, though. Call them. Email them. Google them. Learn as much as possible about them — age, gender, income, location, likes, dislikes, idiosyncrasies, so on and so forth.

Are your readers on Facebook, Twitter or LinkedIn? What about the blogosphere? Wherever they hang out, use social media to find them, then walk in their shoes. The more you understand them, the easier it'll be for you to speak their language and help them understand why they should be doing business with your client.

4. Develop strong presentation skills.

It's one thing to be able to write well. It's quite another to be able to present your work with the utmost confidence and conviction. But some of the most successful copywriters I've met over the years have had as much command of the spoken as the written word.

Those with strong presentation skills are more effective in selling their work to both their colleagues and clients. They're also given more opportunities to attend important meetings, speak at conferences and assume positions of leadership.

If you're uncomfortable speaking in front of an audience, consider joining Toastmasters International, a nonprofit educational organization that helps people improve their public speaking, communication and leadership skills.

As I wrote here on this blog more than six years ago (May 17, 2004)...

Back in the day, one of my dreams was to hone my public speaking skills to the point where I could lead seminars and speak at conferences and industry events about direct marketing and creativity. At the time (in the late '80s), the extent of my public speaking opportunities was only a couple of wedding toasts — admittedly, fair to middling "best man" mumbo jumbo — so if I was ever going to make it to the big leagues, I knew I needed to take more swings of the bat. I knew I needed Toastmasters. That was then. Now, looking back, I can unequivocally say that more than five years of experience as a Toastmaster — including two stints as club president and more than several rounds of speech contests — went a long way toward changing my life, instilling in me the confidence and skills necessary for all the speaking I do nowadays part and parcel of my career.

There's no question that I enjoy my role as a professional copywriter. But I also take pride in my abilities as a presenter. Developing my own skills as a public speaker was one of the best things I've done for my career so far. Being able to present has not only helped me sell my own work, it's helped me enhance my personal brand and led to countless opportunities I wouldn't have had otherwise.

5. Keep your head out of the sand.

It's no coincidence that some of the best copywriters in the business have eclectic tastes and varied interests. When they're not hunkered down on the job, sequestered under tight deadline pressure, they're taking in all that life has to offer as both spectators and participants.

They're bookworms, moviegoers, sightseers and pop culture junkies, people with insatiable appetites for news and information. They're social butterflies, night owls and day-trippers, free-spirited individuals who are curious by nature.

They read everything from best-selling business books to celebrity gossip blogs.

They watch everything from game shows to talk shows, Mad Men to Desperate Housewives, sitcoms to soap operas, reality TV to Glee.

They do everything from hiking and biking to attending concerts, fundraisers, sporting events, museums and the theater.

They try almost anything from newly opened restaurants to ri-
diculously offbeat adventure vacations.

The bottom line is that to be successful as a copywriter over the
course of a career, you can't be reclusive and introverted. You
need to have a breadth of knowledge and experience in order to
write about a broad range of topics and issues. You need to keep
your head out of the sand and your fingers on the pulse of what's
happening in the world today.

6. Exercise good judgment.

A copywriter has meetings to attend and research to conduct,
but the majority of his or her work hours are spent, well, writing
copy — and often under the pressure of exceedingly high expec-
tations and incredibly tight deadlines.

Talent is important. But so is good judgment. Whatever you're
writing, you have to have both the experience and intuition to
choose just the right words for the assignment time after time.

You also have to decide for yourself when to let go of your work
and share it with your colleagues and clients.

As Roger von Oech writes on page 110 of his book, "A Kick In The
Seat Of The Pants"...

"The judge performs the evaluation function of the creative pro-
cess. When you adopt this role, you decide what to do with the
idea: implement it, modify it, or discard it completely. In carrying
out this task, you should recognize imperfections in the new idea
without overstating them. You should also be open to interesting
possibilities and use your imagination to develop these without
losing your sense of reality and perspective." [10]

7. Meet your deadlines.

If you've been around the block once or twice as a copywriter, you
know better than to think anyone's going to just give you enough
time to do your very best work. You have to make the time.

197

Yup. Over the course of my career, I've rarely seen a schedule that permits a copywriter the luxury of putting in the time he or she would really like to dedicate to a project.

Every assignment is a rush. Everything is due yesterday. That's the nature of advertising and marketing, the bane of a copywriter's existence. That's the one thing you have to understand if you want to succeed in this business.

Incredibly tight deadlines come with the territory. And those deadlines had better be met.

That doesn't mean you can't ask for an extension if you don't have enough time to finish an assignment. But if you want to establish a reputation as a reliable, low-maintenance copywriter, the wordsmith to go to for high-quality work that's on time, every time, don't make it a habit.

There's a reason why so many copywriters are accustomed to burning the candle at both ends.

Deadlines.

No, copywriting is not a nine to five job. It's a matter of jumping through hoops and going the extra mile. It's a demanding profession and stressful occupation, a serious commitment you make to your colleagues and clients.

8. Be a team player.

Most copywriters are accustomed to working alone, sequestered away from the rest of the team, doors closed, blinds drawn, working feverishly against time.

It's what we do out of necessity, when there's no room for distractions and we just need to put our heads down to get the job done as soon as possible.

Yet while it's certainly not unusual for a copywriter to do his or her thing in isolation, battling loneliness as well as the clock, it really shouldn't be the norm.

Sure, to succeed as a copywriter, you need to be a self-starter, capable of working independently for long stretches of time. But you also need to be a team player, someone who works well with others — especially designers, creative directors and account people — and can appreciate the importance of timely, seamless handoffs between everyone involved in a project.

You need to be disciplined enough to work in a vacuum (if necessary), but you don't want to be an introvert. The more enthusiastically you collaborate and communicate with others, the better.

If you're invited to a meeting, be punctual and prepared to participate.

If you're taking changes to your work, respond promptly and positively.

If you're given a deadline, beat it.

Brainstorm — or just plain socialize — with your colleagues and clients as much as possible. Get away from your desk and out of your office whenever the opportunity presents itself.

If you go out of your way to show your support for those who depend on you, they'll be more likely to return the favor and do everything they can to ensure your success.

9. Sweat the small stuff.

It's one thing to be a creative genius, to be that extra special someone in the room who can come up with surprisingly brilliant ideas practically on demand, time and time again.

That's the glamour and glory of the business.

But the consummate copywriter is actually a stickler for details, someone who's as strong on the left side of the brain as the right, who's as analytical and obsessive as conceptual and extemporaneous, who's as aware of the importance of being an accurate, fact-based tactician as much as an original, award-winning craftsperson.

That part of the job is not as exciting as it is necessary.

Yes, it's not good enough to be just a great wordsmith and marketer. If you want to earn a living as a copywriter, you also have to be a good researcher and project manager, an avid reader and a competent verbal communicator, someone who can appreciate the fact that a great deal of your success depends on your ability to wear a variety of other hats well when you're not actually writing.

To sweat the small stuff means to be punctual and deadline-oriented, to ask the right questions and make the right points during meetings and presentations.

It also means to be a good proofreader and gatekeeper. So don't count on someone else to catch your mistakes. Be your own worst critic. Use a spell-checking program. And keep a dictionary on your desk. Scrupulously review every single word you write before you turn it over to the powers that be. After all, nothing can undermine your credibility as a copywriter faster than a typo or misspelling.

10. Use social media.

A copywriter's job is to use the written word to promote something or someone using a variety of media, anything from radio to TV, direct mail to email, websites to billboards, print ads to assorted signage, sky writing, you name it.

And today, included among all that tried-and-true, traditional media are blogs, Facebook, Twitter and other popular Internet-based, self-publishing vehicles.

The fact is, anyone working in the marketing, advertising, sales and PR fields who knows how to use social media tools and technologies will likely be much more successful amidst this new communications era.

And those who earn a living writing copy have an obvious competitive advantage. After all, the better you write, the better chance you have of stringing together the right messages for the right occasions and making yourself heard loud and clear above the social media din.

So use social media — but not just on behalf of your clients and customers, on behalf of yourself, too.

Social media is the ideal forum for a copywriter. It's where you can network with other like-minded professionals, keep up on breaking news and learn from industry gurus. It's also where you can share your own knowledge and expertise, where you can actually practice — and demonstrate — your craft in public.

Writing tweets, blog posts, status updates, notes and anything else in social media not only keeps your writing fresh, it keeps you up to speed on the latest communications platforms. It's a great way to connect with the modern world and succeed as a copywriter in today's day and age.

[1] Godin, Seth. *Meatball Sundae: Is Your Marketing Out of Sync?* The Penguin Group. 2007

[2] Clark, Brian. "10 Effective Ways to Get More Blog Subscribers." *Copyblogger.* https://copyblogger.com/10-effective-ways-to-get-more-blog-subscribers/

[3] Hatch, Denny and Jackson, Don. *2,239 Tested Secrets For Direct Marketing Success: The Pros Tell You Their Time-Proven Secrets.* McGraw Hill, 1999.

[4] Morrissey, Brian. "Cause Marketing Meets Social Media." *Adweek.* May 18, 2009

[5] Kanter, Beth. "Cause Marketing or Cause Me To Puke Marketing? Interview with Scott Henderson." *Beth's Blog: Nonprofits and Social Media.* https://beth.typepad.com/beths_blog/2009/05/cause-marketing-or-cause-me-to-puke-marketing-interview-with-scott-henderson.html

[6] O'Malley, Gavin. "Conventional Cause Marketing Evolves Via Social Media." *Online Media Daily.* March 15, 2009. https://www.mediapost.com/publications/article/101916/conventional-cause-marketing-evolves-via-social-me.html

[7] Hatch, Denny and Jackson, Don. *2,239 Tested Secrets For Direct Marketing Success: The Pros Tell You Their Time-Proven Secrets.* McGraw Hill, 1999.

[8] Godin, Seth. *The Dip: A Little Book That Teaches You When to Quit (and When to Stick).* Portfolio. 2007

[9] Covey, Stephen R. *The Seven Habits of Highly Effective People.* Simon & Schuster. 1989

[10] Von Oech, Roger. *A Kick in the Seat of the Pants: Using Your Explorer, Artist, Judge, and Warrior to Be More Creative.* William Morrow. 1986

LESSON 18

DO *WELL* BY *DOING* GOOD

LESSON 18, DO WELL BY DOING GOOD

IT IS REWARDING TO WORK ON BEHALF OF NONPROFIT ORGANIZATIONS AND WORTHY CAUSES. MAKING MONEY IS ONE THING, MAKING A DIFFERENCE IS ANOTHER. TAKE ADVANTAGE OF THE OPPORTUNITY TO HELP OTHERS WHILE HELPING YOURSELF, TOO.

2010-2013

That someone, who helped me get back on my feet, in this case, was Catherine. Out of the blue, I got a call from her. She's someone I knew from my involvement in the New England Direct Marketing Association, and someone I looked up to with great admiration as a direct marketing professional.

There was an immediate opening at the company she worked at in Lexington, Massachusetts, ironically right down the street from where I worked at Job 16. Could I come in for an interview?

That wasn't even a question. After that interview with Catherine and another round of interviews with her colleagues, it was only a matter of a little back-and-forth before I found myself working at another agency that specialized in direct response fundraising, not at all unlike a couple other jobs I had in the past.

To say this new job opportunity came at the right time would be an understatement. I considered myself a lucky man, someone who felt indebted to not just Catherine, but to the three partners who ran this organization, George, Phillip and Adam.

I was a creative director responsible for writing a ton of direct mail for a few of the most renowned charitable organizations in the world, including Habitat for Humanity, the Alzheimer's Association and the American Diabetes Association. This was running with the big dogs, not a gig for the faint of heart and thin-skinned, as the pressure was on to produce top-shelf creative work under tight deadline pressure on a consistent basis.

There was also a lot of travel, at least compared to most of my other jobs. I would join forces with a team of account people, those who were responsible for working directly with the clients, for a trip to, say, Atlanta, Chicago, or Washington, D.C, usually to pitch our work or present a campaign.

I put my all into that job, overall. I gave them my very best effort. In fact, I feel I did some of the best writing I had done in quite a long time while I worked here. It was very fulfilling work, too, as the causes we represented were exemplary to say the least.

While the work was mostly direct mail in some print, there was a little bit of email and even some social media incorporated into the mix. In fact, we won a very prestigious MITX (the Massachusetts Innovation and Technology Exchange) award for a social media campaign we did for Birthright Israel, a project to which I was a significant, not huge contributor. It involved a Pinterest contest where we asked their donors to pin pictures of their kids' bar or bat mitzvahs as a way of entering to win.

Being honored at the MITX awards was a big deal, as many of the big, well—known agencies in Boston entered their work in this competition. I have won a lot of awards for my copywriting, creative direction and even social media, but most of those honors have been from the New England Direct Marketing Association. This was a novelty, an especially impressive feat. Good for us. I felt fortunate.

While the work I was doing there was incredibly fulfilling, a fun, little perk was the fact that the company had a kitchen stocked with free food. So, at lunch, many employees would gather there and make their lunch, just like you might at home with your family. This was just one of many benefits of working among the very positive corporate culture there.

Another highlight of my time as a member of this agency team was being able to partner with an extremely talented designer, Dan. Dan's office was next to mine, so we worked together quite a bit. He was a true professional, a very quiet and unassuming man, but someone who had a great deal of experience specializing in direct mail design for nonprofit organizations. He had won a lot of awards, too, for the projects he worked on, so whenever I worked with him, I was confident that what we did together would not just read well, but look ridiculously awesome.

I also had the chance on a few occasions to bring in a freelancer to handle some of the overflow work. I called on Eric, a veteran wordsmith who had done work for me at several other places in the past. Eric is not only an industry veteran and a highly skilled copywriter he's also a great guy and so easy to work with. I couldn't have been happier to give him the opportunity to work on a good handful of projects while I was at this agency.

To this day, every December, Eric sends me an email to wish me happy holidays that includes pictures of some of the fish he caught during the course of the past year. He's such a nice guy, someone who seems to have a good work-life balance and certainly a great way with people.

I have only fond memories of my time working at this agency.

Wait! What? I can't tell a lie. There is one incident that occurred — that had nothing to do with the agency and everything to do with me — while I was working there that I wish I could forget.

Yes, the time I thought I could be dying, and my life flashed before my eyes. Seriously.

I was at my desk talking to an intern who had been working there for a few months, when all of a sudden I became violently ill. I literally fell off my chair onto the floor and started throwing up, shaking, yelling and screaming. I felt like the world was going to end. My world.

I'm not exaggerating. I had never experienced anything like this before, not even close.

People around me who, thankfully, rushed into my office to help me must have been shaken up. I remember a lot of colleagues — especially my boss, Catherine — around me talking and doing everything they could to help, and then all of a sudden I was being taken by ambulance to the hospital.

I was out of it for a few hours, conscious, but as sick as I have ever been for that length of time. Turns out it was a severe case of vertigo, which had foreshadowed itself for a few weeks leading up to that episode. I had noticed I had been feeling a little bit dizzy from time to time, but never in my wildest imagination thought I would have become that sick… and actually survive.

That extraordinarily frightening event passed about as quickly as it came, like I said, lasting only a few hours. But honestly that felt like an interminably long time. After a battery of tests, doctors could not figure out what had happened, outside of the fact that it was vertigo. And so, after a few days of convalescence, I eventually returned to work.

But I honestly never felt the same there again. I was a little embarrassed to have shown such vulnerability and weakness to my colleagues, even though the vertigo was clearly beyond my control.

I also began to think more of my own mortality and what I really wanted to do in my career. While this was an excellent job I had there, it was mostly direct mail, something I thought I had left behind me years ago for the new wave of digital marketing and social media.

I continued to give this job, Job 18, everything I had, but I knew that a change of scenery might do me good. I can't thank the good people at this firm for being such outstanding colleagues and teammates while I was there, especially during those last few months when I wasn't feeling 100%. I was proud to work with them and am grateful for the opportunity I had to contribute to the company's success.

I had a tremendous final stretch run with this blue-chip agency, until after the holidays when I decided to move on away from direct mail and fundraising to hopefully get back into doing more work online including social media.

4 LESSONS MARKETERS CAN LEARN FROM LOCAL TV NEWS REPORTERS

This post was initially published on BostInnovation on July 28, 2011. To read the original post there, click here.

Today — thanks to social media, smartphones and other new digital communications platforms and tools — what the savviest of consumers are asking of their favorite brands is almost as much as they'd expect from their best friends and family. They want your time, support and undivided attention — and they want it at their convenience. It's not just due to modern technology, though. It's a bold, new sense of entitlement that's been enthusiastically adopted by those on the receiving end of your messages.

In this era in which the corporation has ceded control — albeit reluctantly — to the customer, businesses can't afford to be seen as out of touch, behind the times or just plain unavailable. How do marketing professionals who are both behind the scenes and on the front lines of the brands they represent adapt to, if not embrace, such a monumental paradigm shift?

Here's one thought. Study the communications styles and strategies of some of the most popular television news report-

ers in Boston, men and women who seem to always be on the cutting-edge when it comes to connecting with a demanding audience. Here are four lessons you can learn from these folks and act on immediately across all of your marketing channels.

1. Have a flair for the dramatic. Like WHDH 7NEWS reporters Dan Hausle, Ryan Schulteis and Susan Tran and their colleagues do, tell a good story whenever you have the opportunity. Unlike them, however, you don't have to be covering a bad accident, a huge fire or a serious crime to capture people's attention. In and of itself, your product or service should be news-worthy enough. Whatever you're pitching, wherever you're pitching it, use emotional, descriptive language to get your points across effectively and make your brand stand out in a competitive marketplace.

2. Don't miss a beat. Take advantage of the fact that breaking news is so hard to ignore. Nonprofit organizations have always done this especially well, either asking for text donations or sending telegram-like direct mail fundraising packages that impart a sense of urgency as soon as possible after natural disasters. But current events don't have to be related to your business in order for you to share them with your constituency and benefit from the exposure. Leveraging social media, any organization can act like a broadcaster and provide live, real-time news updates that will help call attention to your brand.

3. Put a smiling face on your brand. Long gone are the days when the public will hang on every word said about your company. Even if what you have to offer is the best thing since sliced bread, it just isn't that simple anymore. There are too many reasons to tune you out. If people aren't too busy to listen to you, they're either skeptical or easily distracted — and yes, quick to exercise their many options. That's why you need to put personality into your promotion and a smiling face on your brand. It's even good to laugh it up once in while. Watch Gene Lavanchy, Kim

208

Carrigan, Elizabeth Hopkins, Doug VB Goudie, and Cindy Fitzgibbon on the FOX 25 Morning News. They don't take themselves too seriously. Yet they're talented, charismatic and extraordinarily good at their craft, perfect role models, if you ask me, for anyone who's trying to win over an audience.

4. Engage with your audience. For the same reason television news reporters interview bystanders on the scene of a big story, ask viewers to share photos (see the WBZ-TV Weather Watchers, for a good example) and talk to their fans on Twitter, marketers should be mingling with their own constituents. Ask your customers and prospects to post product reviews, eyewitness reports and other forms of consumer-generated media online. It behooves you to receive such direct, honest perspectives from those whose attention you covet. But there's another, perhaps even more important, reason to interact with the public. Commerce has gone social. People are talking about you (online and off), whether you like it or not. So it pays to inject yourself into those conversations and — ideally — win more friends in the process.

THE IMPORTANCE OF LINKEDIN RECOMMENDATIONS

Given my outgoing personality, my obsession with the latest news and the fact that I've always been an early adopter of new communications tools, it's no surprise that I've been enamored with social media from the get-go.

I can't tell you how excited I was to launch my own blog in early 2004, where I've written nearly 100,000 words on almost anything and everything that has to do with marketing. I became a member of Facebook in late 2007. I joined Twitter on May 8, 2008. I've bookmarked over 4,800 blog posts and articles on

Delicious. I use Google Reader on a regular basis. And I have my own YouTube channel, which I use to share my thoughts on what's important to me — and, hopefully, others — in the industry in which I earn my livelihood.

But out of all the social media outposts where I've established a presence, the one that probably gets the most attention among traditional business folks is LinkedIn, which I joined on July 26, 2004, almost seven years ago. In fact, I'm proud to say I was among the first one million members — number 882,759, to be exact — of this professional networking site that recently eclipsed the 100 million-member mark.

On LinkedIn, I'm fortunate to have connected with over 800 others, people who, like me, are more than happy to help one another make the most of their professional lives. And that includes writing recommendations for those among your network who deserve to be singled out for their expertise and experience.

So far, I've written recommendations for 59 people in my LinkedIn network, each of whom I've worked with in some capacity during the course of my career. I'm grateful for the 44 recommendations that others have written for me.

LinkedIn recommendations should be short and to the point, speaking to the strengths and skills you've seen up close and personal in the recipients of your high praise. When you write one, try to be as specific as possible, providing your own unique perspective on why someone else should be interested in hiring or doing business in some capacity with this individual. If he or she is a star, say so, enthusiastically and effusively. Cite his or her attributes and actual accomplishments. Use colorful adjectives and descriptive prose. You want to sound like you mean every single one of your kind words, not like you wrote them just because you were asked.

In fact, not every one of your LinkedIn recommendations needs to be solicited. Write one or two every once in a while for those who especially stand out. They'll not only thank you for it, the likelihood is they'll reciprocate and write a recommendation for you in return. That's certainly good form.

And, yes, while it may be a little awkward, don't worry about declining someone's request to write a recommendation if for any reason you think it's unwarranted. That's business.

The bottom line is that whether you're providing them for others or receiving them yourself, LinkedIn recommendations are extremely important. They're a big part of your social currency that should reflect well on you as a corporate citizen and go a long way toward enhancing your online reputation.

To read all 59 of the LinkedIn recommendations I've written so far, please check out my LinkedIn profile by clicking here.

And...what about you? How many LinkedIn recommendations have you written and received? If you have anything to add to this post, please don't hesitate to leave a comment below.

IF WE'RE TALKING ABOUT SOCIAL MEDIA, WE'RE TALKING ABOUT A REVOLUTION

Thanks to the crazy amount of time I spend talking to others about blogs, Twitter, Facebook, LinkedIn and the like, I've had plenty of opportunities to hear practically every reason in the book why some people still haven't jumped on the social media bandwagon.

Many of these folks claim there aren't enough hours in the day for them to be spending any more time online, while others say they just don't understand how to use these new digital tools and technologies.

My own personal theory is that a good percentage of these lag-gards and stragglers are more concerned about their privacy than they care to admit, afraid of revealing themselves so openly and publicly across the social web.

But to all of these people, I don't know what to say anymore than what I've already said time and again to anyone within earshot about the countless benefits of using social media to engage with customers and constituents, friends and family.

Using social media, you can establish long-term, mutually-ben-eficial relationships with people you might never have gotten to know otherwise.

You can learn more than you would imagine from complete and utter strangers.

And if you know how to work a crowd, you can find yourself front and center, informing and entertaining your own rapt audience, a tribe of devoted fans and followers who hang on your every word.

But anything I've ever said about the efficacy of social media as vehicles for powerful communications pales in comparison to the impact of watching Social Media Video 2013, a cool, new video from Eric Qualman on the prevalence and popularity of social media around the world.

LESSON 19 WORK HARD PLAY HARD

LESSON 19, WORK HARD, PLAY HARD
GIVE YOUR JOB EVERYTHING YOU GOT AND THEN SOME. PUT IN LONG HOURS. BE WILLING TO GO ABOVE AND BEYOND. HAVE FUN WITH YOUR COLLEAGUES, TOO. THE MORE YOU GET TO KNOW EACH OTHER PERSONALLY, NOT JUST PROFESSIONALLY, THE BETTER YOU'LL WORK TOGETHER AS A TEAM.

2013-2017

I freelanced for a while before landing my next full-time job. I set up my home office in a spare bedroom, where I had a view of the yard where my kids — Scott, Ben, David and Sophie — used to play. They were grown up for the most part at this time. Only one of them still lived at home. Ben, our youngest, was still in high school. His older brother, Scott, had moved out of the house shortly after he graduated from Lincoln-Sudbury Regional High School and was working as a carpenter and playing drums in a reggae band. My stepchildren — Sophie and David, my wife Barbara's children from her first marriage — are about 10 years older, so they were long gone from living under the same roof with us.

I got a few small projects to work on as a soloist, but I needed something full-time. I reached out to Nicholas, someone I knew from my involvement in the New England Direct Marketing Association. About ten years younger than me, he and I had led relatively similar parallel professional lives in the same industry, although he had achieved much more success. He was someone I regarded as a digital marketing genius and consummate businessman. He had founded his own digital marketing agency years ago, and I always thought working for him would be a natural fit for me.

I was soon to find out if that was the case because, yes, fortunately, he had some work for me. He needed a writer to pull together regular social media content for a big, important client of his. It wasn't full-time work, but it was a foot in the door, even though it didn't actually require me to be on-site. My primary responsibility was to manage this client's social media channels, keeping them as active as possible on a frequent basis. I needed to provide strategy and report on results, but the bulk of my time was spent writing, scheduling and publishing, all with the intent of growing this account in mind.

I was in — at least partway.

Sure enough, after just a couple months or so, he did bring me in as his director of social media. The full-time role had me managing a small team of specialists. Our collective responsibility was to provide content and analyses on behalf of a handful of the agency's clients.

It was a great gig, and certainly one that was in my domain. I had been determined to make social media my career focus for a long time. This was my opportunity, and really the first time in my professional journey that my role was not centered around traditional copywriting and the creative department. I would be spending the bulk of my time on Twitter, Facebook, Instagram, LinkedIn, You-Tube and the like, not on direct mail or even email.

I had a very nice office at this agency in Allston, Massachusetts. After another frustrating, long commute every morning, it felt good to sit down behind my desk and to be surrounded by four walls. This was a modicum of creature comforts I got to enjoy, the spoils of being a manager, I suppose.

It was during my time working here that I began to realize just how powerful it was to use video on social media.

I would quite frequently go outside during lunch and take a walk around the surrounding neighborhoods, jumping onto Periscope to record a live video on Twitter. I would talk about social media, marketing and whatever came to mind. I'd watch how many followers I got and occasionally even interact with them. These walking and talking videos came instinctively to me. If I could take doing these to the next level, perhaps monetizing my efforts...now that would be nice.

Not all these videos I recorded were live, either. I would sometimes sit down on a bench and use the selfie mode on my camera to talk about the same topics, just more rehearsed and less impromptu, sharing them at a later time on social media.

Not that I wouldn't change up the topics from time to time. For instance, prior to my 40th high school reunion, I went down memory lane, expressing my thoughts about days gone by on video, publishing it afterwards on the class's Face-book page. Many of my former classmates brought up that video in conversation at the reunion, further reinforcing to me just how compelling, if not irresistible, video was in our lives now as a communications medium.

My side gig as a videographer, or vlogger, if you will, originated during these years. Not that I was doing any of this on the job. It was all on my own time, during lunch or in the evening. Often on the weekends, too. This was my passion, almost an obsession. I had a hunch that video was only going to get bigger as a medium. I wanted to be in at the beginning of this emerging trend.

Today, my YouTube channel includes over 300 videos I have recorded on the subject of social media and around the same amount that are motivational, most of which have been done in the last few years.

At Job 19, I encouraged Nicholas to invest more time into video. I told him how great he would be at it. He's a naturally gifted speaker and an infinite fountain of knowledge when it comes to anything to do with digital marketing. He has recorded some clips here and there, all of which are absolutely fantastic. I believe strongly in the power and possibilities of video, especially matched with such an authoritative, knowledgeable leader as him.

Easily the best opportunity to present itself to me while I was at this agency was Nicholas asking me to take over him as a writer for ClickZ, a massive online resource of interactive marketing news. Not only did I have a great deal of autonomy in this role, but I also had a sizable audience of readers. I could write about almost anything I wanted to as long as it was regarding social media. What could be better?

During my tenure as a contributor to ClickZ, I published some 30 articles or so, all of which I repurposed on both the agency blog and my own. We got a great deal of mileage out of those pieces, sharing them as much as possible across social media platforms like Twitter, LinkedIn and Facebook.

The agency blog was something I really liked about working at this agency. The people who worked here made it a priority, talking about it at our weekly meetings and urging employees to contribute to it. This was right up my alley, so between all those ClickZ articles and anything I would write especially for the blog, I was chalking up a ton of good content on behalf of my employer.

Those weekly meetings sure kept us on our toes, by the way. We would review critical agency business and share news and information with each other, but we would also have some good, long, deep conversations about corporate culture and even personal goings-on. I particularly enjoyed the many opportunities I had to present to everyone present at these meetings about what was going on in the world of social media. Our time spent together regularly in one conference room went a long way toward building camaraderie and an incredibly positive team morale.

I was also writing thousands of tweets. Yes, literally thousands. That was a big part of what we did as a social media team. We kept our clients' social media channels populated with all the words and pictures we could create. We wrote about their products and services, their industries, their employees, you name it. Anything to do with their business was potential fodder for their followers on social media.

This work was as much a challenge as it was repetitive. I was very happy to be immersed in social media on a full-time basis, but honestly, it was almost too much. It was exhausting at times. It was constant dotting the i's and crossing the t's, managing a multitude of details and tasks. When you're doing that much of any one thing, it's hard to see the forest for the trees, to appreciate what you enjoy about the work without feeling stressed out and tired.

The company outings that took place here a few times a year were ridiculously awesome. So much fun. We did everything from having a scavenger hunt in the woods in a torrential rainstorm, to sailing on a tall ship around Boston harbor, to spending time at the 21-degree ice bar at Faneuil Hall Marketplace where we all stood around enjoying a cold (very cold) beverage or two and shivering in heavy winter coats. We also went to one of those cool, indoor trampoline parks, where I had fun doing somersaults and playing dodgeball, but pulled a muscle that forced me to take off six weeks of training for the upcoming Boston Marathon. Ouch.

This period of my life did take a personal toll on me. Having nothing to do with my employer, but coinciding with my time there, I was diagnosed with a rare case of trigeminal neuralgia, which is acute facial pain that can come and go, but when it comes, it hurts terribly.

It would come on me several times a day, only for a few minutes at a time, but when I felt it, I had to make sure to not wince in public.

I had it for four or five months or so before it was diagnosed, after which time I at least knew what it was and was prepared for it when it struck. I still deal with it today, but have it very much under control.

There was also a recurrence of the vertigo I had experienced in 2012. Over the course of a long weekend in 2014, away from the office, I had another serious attack of this crazy thing that resulted in another trip to the emergency room by ambulance. I had fallen ill while shopping alone in Marshall's. I mean fallen. I literally fell to the floor, almost completely incapacitated. Sick as a dog. This was just two days before I was scheduled to run yet another Boston Marathon, too. Unbelievably, I recovered quite quickly and was able to go the full 26.2-mile distance successfully that Patriots' Day.

Then there were the car accidents, the three different times I was rear-ended during my long morning commute, two times only slightly, but one of those happened on the Mass Pike. I was stuck in stop-and-go traffic and could see in my rear-view mirror a large SUV-like vehicle — maybe it was a pick-up truck, I can't recall — the driver of which did not seem to be paying attention. Sure enough, he hit me so hard from behind that my car was totaled. I was upset, to say the least, but thankfully only suffered a minor case of whiplash.

I was also concerned about my father's failing health. He was such a strong, determined man, but time was catching up to him. If it wasn't one health setback, it was another, and I couldn't stop worrying about him.

Fortunately, there were countless things I enjoyed about the experience of working at this blue-chip highly acclaimed agency.

No matter which department you were working with, the people there were fantastic. Creative. SEO. Analytics. Sales. Web development. Media. Client service. Operations. You name it.

Nicholas had founded this company in 2001 with two others, Stan and Bill, and the three of them made up an ideal brain trust, smart as can be, steady as a rock, a tour de force when it comes to agency acumen and leadership. I looked up to this trio with admiration and respect, impressed with their success, amazed at their accomplishments.

Three cheers for them for building such a remarkable place of employment for so many digital marketing professionals over so many years.

I loved being a full-time employee here in the burgeoning social media space. I was proud to be managing such a talented team of hard-working professionals. Writing articles on a regular basis for ClickZ and the agency blog was extremely satisfying, a real joy. I was incredibly proud to be earning a livelihood in such a cool, cutting-edge work environment.

Hey, did I mention all the delicious healthy snacks that were available in the kitchen anytime we liked? Protein bars, chips, nuts and occasionally on a Friday afternoon, pizza and cold beverages. What could be better?

One of my finer moments here, if I do say so myself, was when I had the opportunity to introduce Nicholas as the New England Direct Marketing Associations Direct Marketer of the Year in 2016, the same award I had been presented with in

2009. It was all about Nicholas, of course — who again, is a genius, if you ask me, when it comes to digital marketing, an incomparable star in the industry — but I was under a lot of pressure in my personal life, to put it mildly, so I took extra special pride in the development and delivery of my speech.

I gave the speech of my life if you ask me, in presenting Nicholas with that prestigious award, one that was so well deserved and a long time coming. It was just a few days after my dear dad had passed at the age of 90 and just a few days before his funeral. Simultaneously, while grieving my father's loss, I was nothing if not focused on the almost monumental task at hand.

I did my job.

But the stress took its toll. I was anxious. I was tense. I was sick to my stomach almost every night, unable to keep my food down after dinner due to anxiety and emotional fatigue. I was beside myself, overwhelmed with grief over my father's departure from this earth while being disappointed that all of the hard work I had put in up to this juncture of my career hadn't, in my mind, exactly paid off.

Like everywhere else I had been employed, I lived and breathed everything I did on the job here, Job 19. I was pushing boundaries. I was going above and beyond. I was embracing a revolutionary, new way of communicating online, and I was using both sides of my brain.

Yes, you see, while I was creating a ton of content for our clients, leveraging the right side of my brain, I was also responsible for producing monthly reports, which tapped the other side of my brain.

Using Excel and crunching numbers was never my bailiwick, so this was new to me. I was working harder than ever, knowing my opportunity to do work in such an exciting, transformative discipline depended on my ability to think analytically. Yikes.

I did it, though. I came through in flying colors if I do say so myself. I worked there just shy of four years, giving everything I had to the company's success. It was the job of my career so far, a significant milestone in my mind. I had added new skills to my repertoire and worked alongside some of the best pros in the business.

I learned so much from my boss, Nicholas, and my colleagues on the leadership team there, people who were clearly second to none in the industry in which I have earned my livelihood.

The workload was demanding and I often felt a lot of pressure, but the opportunities I was given there to write, manage, speak and lead were practically unprecedented up to that point in my career.

Working at this agency, Job 19, I felt like I was part of something big, an accelerating force of teamwork that knew no bounds when it came to professional success. I put in very long hours, but I have done that at all of my jobs. To come out ahead there, you had to be both talented and tenacious, two qualities I knew I shared with my fellow employees.

It wasn't the first time I made the decision to move on without having another full-time job lined up. What else is new, right? But I did have some part-time contract work in the queue, never mind the fact that I wanted to try being my own boss again, similar to what I had going for me back in the early to mid 90s.

Leaving this job felt anti-climactic given the fact that I had worked there for so long (for me) and had buried myself so deeply in the work, my clients and our corporate culture. I had mixed feelings about saying goodbye, as it was — at least on paper — a dream job for me. There were so many things I enjoyed about what I did at this agency and collaborating with the good people there, but the stress I was feeling — both personally and professionally — was something I knew I had to put behind me, one way or another.

So, once again, I found myself taking that daunting, dangerous walk on the high wire without a safety net below.

All blog posts in this chapter, Chapter 19, were written by Bob Cargill for ClickZ.com and the Overdrive Interactive blog and are republished here with permission.

10 WAYS A PERSONAL BRAND ON SOCIAL MEDIA HELPS THE CORPORATE BRAND BEHIND IT

No one can say that there aren't many benefits of having a strong personal brand on social media. After all, your LinkedIn profile is where practically everyone goes to check you out if they're considering doing business with you in any way, shape or form. If you have a few presentations uploaded to SlideShare, a few dozen posts published on a blog and a few hundred followers on Twitter, even better.

Using social media to showcase your background, skills, talent and expertise is a no-brainer.

But the benefits of personal branding on social media aren't limited to the owner of that brand only. Everyone around those who are prevalent and popular online, the "corporate all-stars" of the business world, as Edelman's Steve Rubel so astutely labelled them in 2009, enjoys the fruits of their labor, from direct reports to supervisors, colleagues to clients, partners to employers.

How? Here's how. Here are 10 ways a personal brand on social media works to the advantage of the corporate brand behind it and is a win-win for everyone involved.

__1. Reach.__ A small company may not have a big audience on social media, but it may have a handful of people among its ranks with their own extensive networks. Riding employees' coattails makes sense if they can help get the word out to a broader, perhaps even better, audience. Like a good ripple effect, the more help brands can get from the people who work for them, the further and faster their messages will travel.

__2. Thought Leadership.__ Social media makes it possible for almost anyone to establish themselves as a renowned expert.

All you need is the time, talent and tenacity. Write a blog post. Record a video. Comment here, there and everywhere. Leaders within an organization should be leaders in their industry. From a selfish standpoint, that may be how to ascend the corporate ladder, but that's also how to generously increase the visibility and credibility of the corporate brand behind you.

3. Education. *Anyone who spends more than a modicum of time on social media knows what a treasure trove of educational resources can be found there. Never mind attending conferences and signing up for webinars. Log in to this channel or that one and boom, you're privy to all the news and information that's fit to share. Social media is a living, breathing education on demand, and more often than not it's on the house.*

4. Camaraderie. *Imagine having access to a circle of like-minded professionals, connections you can count on to keep you up to date and in the know, wherever you are, whenever you want. That's social media. People may not pick up the phone when you call or respond to your email, but if you mention them in a tweet or tag them on Facebook, suddenly you have their attention. That's influence. That's clout. That's a big benefit to both personal and corporate brands.*

5. Social Proof. *People are more likely to trust and support other like-minded people, not distant, impersonal corporate logos and brands. When you earn likes, shares and comments as an employee, not only does it go a long way toward establishing a great reputation for your own personal brand, it benefits the corporate brand behind you. Your influence and authority on social media reflects positively on the products and services you represent and can be leveraged by those who employ you.*

6. Inspiration. *We all know the importance of keeping team members properly inspired. While often employers can't afford to send their people to conferences and industry events, they can* easily permit, if not encourage, employees to spend time on social media, listening, learning, reading and writing. Regular exposure to such resources goes a long way toward enabling and empowering people to go above and beyond in their work on behalf of the brands they represent.

7. Scalability. If practice makes perfect, social media is the place to go to hone your skills in the areas of writing, networking, research, thought leadership and branding. For the individual practitioner, work done with these tools and technologies can lead to something more valuable to the brand he or she represents. Status updates can result in potential new customers and clients. Blog posts can be turned into white papers. Time spent on Twitter can yield new findings, data, insights and connections that are ripe to be taken advantage of at an enterprise level.

8. Accountability. Those who are active on social media for business reasons are invariably those who are passionate about their jobs, careers and professions. They are bold, brave, outgoing and engaging, people who are blessed with the qualities associated with leaders, accountable to their respective roles and responsibilities. After all, like speakers, writers, artists, athletes, performers and entertainers, they're putting their reputations on the line every time they share something with others. Their activities are both public and permanent, so they had better know what they're doing or else they're subject to criticism.

9. Networking. They don't call it social media for nothing. The more active you are on LinkedIn, Twitter, Facebook and the like, the more connections you'll amass. Yes, those so-called "corporate all-stars" Steve Rubel referred to have legions of followers, people who can help not just themselves, but the brands they represent. Unless a corporate brand is a household name or a celebrity of some type, it takes a lot of time to build a large, engaged audience. Those with strong personal brands can help their employers get there more quickly by providing access to their own networks and triggering engagement among their constituencies.

10. Authenticity. Even if you are well-known for one reason or another, a corporate logo will only get you so far along the path to long-standing, mutually beneficial relationships with your audience members. The trust factor looms large on social media. That's where a good personal brand enters the picture. Employers can draft behind their employee ambassadors in order to win over new followers and fans, people who will give them much more attention if only due to their confidence in their friends.

The bottom line is that it takes a village to come out ahead on social media. Both personal and corporate brands should take great pains to work together and to realize that we're talking about a collaborative activity, not one that exists in a silo. It pays for employers to not just activate their employees on these channels, but to join them in the conversation.

SIX REASONS DIRECT MARKETERS SHOULD BE SWOONING OVER SOCIAL MEDIA

I'm not going to lie. I get it. I really do get it.

As someone who earned a livelihood for many years writing copy almost exclusively for direct mail and email, I totally understand why some dyed-in-the-wool direct marketers are still on the fence about using social media.

Tweeting, blogging and sharing selfies on Instagram just doesn't have the same appeal to them as launching one of their own targeted, timely campaigns with a strong offer geared toward a qualified audience to which quantifiable metrics can be applied.

They're concerned about ROI and reputation. They're afraid of the risk.

I understand. I feel their pain. After all, I had the same questions and doubts myself when I began blogging in 2004. I wondered how social media was going to blend into the marketing mix effectively. I dealt with the same steep learning curve and challenges. I had to convince my colleagues and clients that time spent on what was then a newfangled means of digital communications didn't mean forgoing traditional best practices.

It was an uphill battle to which there seemed no end.

That was then, this is now, yet I still find myself shouting from the rooftops sometimes that I have seen the future of direct marketing and it includes social media.

Hello.

It's not like I'm suggesting you use social media to the exclusion of other communication channels at your disposal. Not at all. I'm talking about putting together cohesive, seamlessly coordinated integrated direct marketing programs that just don't give short shrift to the relatively new kid on the block.

I'm saying give social media a seat at the table, maybe even at the head of the table every once in while.

I'm asking for a bigger piece of the marketing spend pie.

Social media — Twitter, Facebook, LinkedIn, Instagram, you name it — goes hand in hand with direct marketing. Believe me. It's got it all going on when it comes to building enduring, mutually beneficial relationships between like-minded parties.

Here are six reasons why direct marketers should be swooning over social media:

1. Creativity. *Over the years, I have written literally thousands of tweets, each of which is akin to a headline, subject line or even* *a small ad. Anyone may be able to string together something coherent in 140 characters or less, but not everyone can make those characters move readers to action. That's why creativity is so important on social media. Copy. Design. Visuals. You name it. Every element of not just a tweet, but all kinds of content — from videos to infographics, blog posts to status updates — needs to be massaged and noodled on to the point where the odds are in its favor of standing out among the clutter of competing messages.*

2. Segmentation. *While it may be difficult, if not impossible to message prospects by name and address on social media, you can target your efforts quite precisely via a host of paid advertising options. Demographics such as gender, age, geographical location, interests, industries, even company names are readily available. You can also upload the email addresses of your existing customers to most social media channels and find them that way, not to mention how many opportunities you have to join the conversation as a brand and connect with your constituents one-on-one.*

3. Offers. *One of the distinguishing characteristics of direct marketing versus other forms of advertising is the call to action (CTA) that prompts prospects to read, download, install, watch or even buy something. Which is exactly what direct marketers like me love so much about social media. Branding is incorporated into our activities as is PR, customer service and the like, but our main objective is invariably driving clicks and conversions. What we have to offer are products and services, news and information, knowledge and advice, music and entertainment, you name it, and what we want is for audience members to take some form of action in return.*

4. Timing. *This is where social media has a decided competitive advantage over traditional marketing channels. It's not hard at* *all to determine when and where people are particularly active, never mind how much you can see for yourself by simply jumping on the networks. Using Facebook Insights, Twitter Analytics and other third party tools such as Audiense, Mention, Tweriod, Buffer and Buzzsumo, you can strategically schedule content to be published when your audience is most likely to see it. You can also post on the fly, sharing content extemporaneously during special occasions, events, whenever and wherever the mood strikes or opportunity calls.*

5. Engagement. *Yet another attribute of direct marketing is the fact that it is supposed to be a two-way street, that is, for every outgoing pitch there should be some degree of reciprocity. In fact, a campaign isn't considered successful without those on the receiving end responding favorably to you in some way, shape or form. Sounds a lot like social media, if you ask me, where the sole purpose of communications is to elicit engagement among a practically infinite sea of consumers and brands, friends and foes. You might say that engaging with others on social media is analogous to returning an order form or calling a toll-free phone number in the terrestrial world. Personal or professional, it's the beginning of a relationship that hopefully will grow.*

6. Measurement. *Where the rubber meets the road in direct marketing is where more attention than you may realize is focused in social media. Content counts for something. But results are worth a lot more. Never mind simply leads and sales. From impressions to clicks, likes to comments, followers to subscribers, every possible metric is tracked, measured, analyzed and put into report form. What works well in the social sphere is recycled and repurposed, while what doesn't is history.*

SOCIAL MEDIA: 15 WAYS YOU'RE DOING IT WRONG

Facebook was founded in 2004, Twitter in 2006. Even Instagram's been around for almost five years. So you can't say this stuff is new anymore.

For some strange reason, however, more marketers and brands than not are still struggling to make heads or tails of social media. Whether they're surprisingly misinformed or just plain lost, they're wasting their time and missing the boat. They're failing to take advantage of what may just be the biggest revolution in communications since the printing press.

To say that's unfortunate would be an understatement.

After all, done right, social media marketing can be a big game changer. It can be an incredibly effective way to attract the attention of your target audience, engage with them and curry their favor. Far too many go into it without doing their homework, though, their false assumptions and inexperience undermining any chance they have for a successful social media program.

Are you making these same mistakes? Are you doing it all wrong despite your very best intentions? You most certainly are if anything that follows sounds even remotely familiar.

1. You don't have a plan.

The last thing you want to do is overlook the first thing you should do. Take pause before launch to map out the route you're going to take on social media. Identify your target audience. Research the competition. Determine your objectives. Choose your tools. Develop your content. Then act accordingly. Eat. Sleep. Tweet. Repeat.

2. You're working alone.

While no one is saying you can't be a hit as a solo act on social media, your chances of success are much greater if you belong to a team. There are only so many hats one person can wear well. Strategic direction. Writing. Design. Marketing. Branding. PR. Web development. Analytics. You name it. You'll make a much bigger impact if you divide and conquer.

3. You're not a writer.

Of course, you're not writing the great American novel. Far from it. But the importance of quality content can't be emphasized enough. Even in 140 characters or less, punctuation, grammar and word play reign supreme. Think like a good journalist or copywriter. Better yet, hire one.

4. You're spread too thin.

While it's good to be in more places than one on social media, don't get carried away with the notion. It's better to be active on one or two channels than to be conspicuous in your inconsistency on a handful. Don't try to be all things to all people. Fish where the fish are. Strike a happy medium between quality and quantity.

5. You're a one-trick pony.

Of course, what might be even worse than being all over the place is being painfully predictable. Putting out the same kind of content in the same place day after day is of little interest to those on the receiving end. It's boring. It's monotonous. It's an easy way to lose an audience.

6. You're not posting in real time.

One of the biggest distinguishing characteristics of social media is its real-time nature, the fact that it makes it possible for users to connect with one another instantaneously. Canned content written and scheduled in advance will only get you so far. You'll have greater influence on your constituency if you share extemporaneous news and commentary on at least an occasional basis.

229

7. You're not being yourself.

Don't try to fake it till you make it. Keep it real from the get-go. Transparency and authenticity are not an option on social media. Offer your opinions, not just the facts. Win friends and influence people with refreshing candor. Mean what you say and say what you mean. Put a face on your brand every step of the way.

8. You're not listening.

Don't be the account that only talks about itself. Don't be a self-centered know-it-all. Pay attention to what others are saying not just about you and your brand, but about their own products and services, too. Mine the media for knowledge and expertise as much as mentions, questions, criticism and praise. Thank people for sharing your content and don't forget to return the favor.

9. You're erratic.

Whatever you're doing on social media, do it on a regular basis. Disappear for even just a few days and you'll be testing the loyalty of those who follow you. Your content stream should serve as a virtual extension of you and your brand, leaving an indelibly consistent, not scattershot, impression on your audience.

10. You're careless.

Written communications is far more informal than it was back in the day. But that doesn't excuse you from making typos or blatant grammatical mistakes. Some colloquialism and slang is called for on social media. But so is some measure of decorum and professionalism.

11. You're no fun.

A good sense of humor goes a long way on social media. Accounts that are spirited, playful, irreverent, even mischievous (in a good-natured way) tend to be popular. Don't hesitate to share a few laughs with your followers and fans. Social media works best for brands that take their products and services, not themselves, seriously.

12. You're as bland as milk toast.

It's much better to be safe than sorry on social media, but that doesn't mean you can't go out on a limb once in a while and express your creativity. Be colorful, not controversial. Bold, not brash. Avoid arguments at all costs and always take the high road. But show you have more than just a pulse, show you have a personality.

13. You're not sharing any pictures.

It's no secret that visual content on social media commands attention. It really doesn't matter what kind, either. Stock images. Candid shots. Video. Instagram. Vine. Complement your words with pictures in any way, shape or form and stand out amid the clutter.

14. You're not paying to play.

You may have the most compelling content imaginable, but you still may not be seen by enough people on social media. Organic reach is down. Attention spans are short. The best laid plans can easily go astray without putting at least a small budget behind your efforts.

15. You're ignoring the numbers.

Branding is important, but like any other form of marketing, social media marketing is all about the results. Establish your goals and develop a methodology for measuring your performance. As Stephen Covey wrote in his book, The Seven Habits of Highly Effective People, "begin with the end in mind."

10 LESSONS LEARNED ABOUT SOCIAL MEDIA FROM MY PARENTS

When I give presentations on social media, I often refer to Dale Carnegie's How to Win Friends and Influence People. After all, so much about social media is about building strong relationships with others. And that's what Dale preached as well as anybody, especially in this classic book.

Yet I really only have to look as far as my parents for reference in this case. They may not be on social media, but so much of what I've learned about interpersonal communications I've learned from them.

And that's what it all boils down to on Twitter, Facebook, LinkedIn and the like. The most successful business people and brands on these channels are those that have a knack for engaging effectively with others as human beings.

Sure, it doesn't hurt that they have either a wealth of knowledge and expertise or a line of ridiculously cool products and services. When all is said and done, however, they are simply themselves — which just might be their most endearing quality.

They are like my parents, in a way, who are nothing if not the real deal. Ages 84 and 90, respectively, my mother and father have always been as authentic and unassuming as they come, people I look up to as the embodiment of character in every way, shape and form.

Specifically, here are the lessons I've learned from my parents that can be applied to activities on social media by individuals like you and me as well as small and big brands alike.

1. Be trustworthy.

This should go without saying, of course, but when it comes to sales and promotion, even the best marketers have a tendency to push the edges. Don't even think about it on social media. Ev-

erything should be kept on the up and up. We're not making deals here. We're making friends, followers and fans.

2. Don't brag.

If honesty is the best policy, so is modesty. No one likes braggadocio. A small shameless plug every once in a while is okay. Your audience should be made aware of your strengths and accomplishments. But the more you talk about others, not yourself, the more inclined they'll be to pay attention to what you have to say and to eventually do business with you.

3. Stay positive.

Remember that nobody likes a complainer. It doesn't matter if we're talking about the Internet and not real life. There's no difference anymore. Lift people's spirits with your hope and optimism. Look on the bright side of life. See the glass as always half full. A positive attitude makes everything a lot easier not just for you, but for those around you.

4. Ask questions.

My parents are great conversationalists, always showing concern for what another person has to say. That's why they've had so many long-lasting, mutually beneficial relationships with others over the years. They know that people are happy to share how they feel with you — and that they're even happier if you actually take an interest.

5. Share.

I was taught as a child not to be selfish, to share with others, especially if they were less fortunate than me. While this notion that "sharing is caring" was ingrained in me at an early age, it applies to everybody on social media today. News and opinion, knowledge and information, activities and whereabouts. All of this is great fodder. All of this is what people and brands alike are expected to dole out to their friends, followers and fans.

6. Don't knock others.

If you don't have something good to say, don't say anything at all. I can't be the only one who heard this as a child. Such timeless advice applies to practically every opportunity we have to say something publicly. What you express on social media ties back to your brand. People want to feel good about their interactions with you, not deflated because you're a downer.

7. Be empathetic.

If you're there for your audience, they'll be there for you. Listen to what they have to say. Respond in a supportive, timely fashion. Put yourself in their shoes. What can you say that will make them smile? What can you do to add dazzle to their day? What do you have to offer that will help them get more out of life? An empathetic ear and a kinder, gentler voice will go a long way toward winning over your audience.

8. Play fair.

If you look at social media as an extension of who you are in real life, this lesson is one of the most important. Be a good sport and don't cut corners. Don't step on any toes to get to the top. Be someone others can look up to for your values, principles and moral code. Play well with others. Corporate citizenship counts.

9. Take pictures.

When I was a kid, my dad loved his slide projector. That and stacks of photo albums were how our road trips, family reunions, summer vacations and campouts were documented. Pictures brought us together. And while they're obviously still kind of a big deal, pictures aren't just for families to share in the privacy of their own homes anymore. They're to share with everybody on social media.

10. Look up.

As much as my parents appreciate what I do for a living, they're the first ones to remind me to look up from my electronic devices as often as possible and to enjoy real conversations with real people. I can't argue with them. Not only is it healthy and refreshing to go unplugged, it's actually where most deals are made. Take your online relationships offline. Have lunch together. Play golf. Take a good long walk. Talk to each other face to face. Social media should be a complement to everything else you do as an individual or a brand, not the be-all and end-all.

DON'T THINK TWICE ABOUT DOING VIDEO ON SOCIAL MEDIA

Andy Warhol was right when he said, "In the future, everyone will be world-famous for 15 minutes."

On second thought, maybe he was putting it too mildly. The future has arrived, and thanks to social media everyone now has the opportunity to be famous for an indefinite period of time, not just 15 minutes.

Look at Casie Neistat. Or King Bach. Then there's Amber Mac. Kim Garst. And Jay Baer. I could go on and on. Funny. Serious. Amusing. Smart. The list of people who have become famous thanks to the emergence of social media is as long as it is varied.

Each of these people has done what every corporate brand and business should be doing on YouTube, Twitter, Facebook and the like. They've leveraged both written and visual content to take advantage of these platforms and stand head and shoulders above everybody else when it comes to copping their share of the spotlight. They've shared knowledge and expertise, laughs and entertainment, news and information, facts and opinion. They've put it all on the line in the name of promoting their own personal brands. And they've succeeded in a big way.

What they've done isn't rocket science, though. Nor is it that difficult, as long as you're willing to put in the time. Success in this space is determined as much by tenacity as it is talent. Online video, live or pre-recorded, is incredibly popular, and anyone in business who isn't doing it today is missing a huge opportunity to attract more customers and clients, never mind more fortune and fame.

Unfortunately, most people out there are afraid to be in front of the camera for a multitude of reasons, especially if the shoot has to do with their jobs. It's nerve-wracking to say the least.

But that tune has to change in 2017. Never mind that anyone in senior management should be prepared to take a starring role. If your responsibilities have anything to do with marketing, advertising, PR or social media, you can't afford to be camera-shy in this day and age.

It's not enough to simply muster up the courage to be a talking head, either. Forget trying to win the award for best actor, actress or picture, but don't be afraid to let your guard down and portray the human side of your brand. The authenticity, transparency and immediacy of your videos on social media count more than whoever has the biggest budget or the most sophisticated production values.

Be yourself. Cool, chill. Keep it real. Spontaneous and off-the-cuff. Have an outline in mind before the action starts, but don't risk appearing stilted and stiff by feeling you have to stick to cue cards or a script. Too much preparation will invariably result in a product that is simply too polished to believe.

You're telling a story when you're in front of the camera. You're taking your audience on a trip to the intersection of your world and theirs. Whether you're talking about your products and people, services and successes, interests and insights, you're talking naturally, spontaneously, sincerely and openly. You're talking about something that you have in common with your audience, something they can relate to, something they will gravitate towards and embrace.

According to this Social Times article written by Nicole Teeters...

"It's increasingly the norm for brands to be active on mediums like Snapchat, Instagram Stories, Facebook Live — places where social storytelling is informal and direct. In this environment, brands need to let loose and allow for marketing that is less polished but that will come across as much more genuine."

The irony is that you need to sacrifice the polish for the sake of the credibility of your videos. Homemade recordings are like homemade brownies. Not only are they more appreciated, they're often even better than those you can buy. Whether you do it yourself or not, though, do it without overthinking it, overproducing it, overrehearsing it. Don't think twice about doing video on social media.

LESSON 20 BE HUMBLE

LESSON 20, BE HUMBLE

THERE IS A FINE LINE BETWEEN SUCCESS AND FAILURE. YOU CAN'T HAVE THE GOOD WITHOUT THE BAD. DON'T EVER BE SO FULL OF YOURSELF THAT YOU CAN'T ACCEPT THE HARSH REALITY THAT NOBODY CARES HOW MANY TIMES YOU FALL DOWN. GETTING RIGHT BACK UP IS WHAT COUNTS. COMMIT TO LIFELONG LEARNING AND MAKE THE MOST OF WHAT YOU'VE GOT EVERY STEP OF THE WAY.

I left a great full-time job at Job 19 to pursue contract and freelance opportunities that I knew were out there.

However, things didn't necessarily turn out as I planned, at least not for a while.

I landed one good gig immediately creating content for another digital marketing agency nearby. The work dried up quickly, though, and I was forced to look elsewhere much sooner than I had anticipated.

Fortunately, another opportunity arose before I knew it, writing copy for yet another small agency, this time around lots of direct mail just like the old days.

I wish that that part-time contract, like the first one after Job 20, lasted longer, but it didn't, and after only six months, I found myself bouncing around like a pinball again, working one short contract after another, trying hard to cobble enough client work together to keep up with my monthly bills.

Sometimes who you know is as important — or even more so — than what you know, and this was more true than ever at this stage of my career. Given the large network I had built during the course of my career so far, I never had to go too long in between jobs before landing on my feet again successfully.

So, yes, I had plenty of work to do, but the income was not adding up. I knew I had some extra time on my schedule. I had heard a lot about ride-sharing and believed being a driver was something I could do in between projects, contracts and assignments. So, I went for it and became a driver for the largest ride-sharing company out there.

Never did I ever expect to be picking up strangers and driving them around town while they were heading out to dinner or coming and going from work, but this became my part-time lot in life for a year or so. I actually enjoyed it, although it could be stressful, having to pay attention to the app and trying to stay focused on where you were going, despite having never driven in certain neighborhoods and areas of the city of Boston.

I liked meeting all the different people who would jump into the backseat of my car. Some were very, very friendly, some real quiet. Some were wicked generous, some were arrogant and demeaning.

I only imagined what it would be like to do something like this as a full-time job for life. It sure was humbling.

I took pride in the impression I made as a ride-sharing driver. I would make sure my car was clean inside and out. I was extremely polite. I learned to talk only when I felt the rider wanted to talk, usually keeping quiet unless they started a conversation. I imagined this was how it felt to be an assistant to someone, having to defer to him or her no matter what. The customer is always right. They had the power. I was only the hired help.

But honestly, I was very impressed with how this particular ride-sharing company operated itself. I was amazed at how much demand there was for rides, especially in the city.

Did you know that ride-sharing riders (at least for this company) can rate their drivers? And vice versa? All the ratings I received were five stars. Perfect. Except for one, who I think was just playing games with me. He gave me a zero, which brought my rating down to 4.91.

I worked for a while as a ride-sharing company driver, here and there, when I needed the money and had the time, but I haven't done it in a few years or so. I hope I never have to do it again.

I learned driving for this company that there are many different situations in life that many of us have to endure, and you just have to realize your place, accept it and make the most of it.

On the days that I would be driving, I would have a whole pregame ritual. I would usually clean out my car and wipe down the windows. I would put water and snacks out for my riders. I would drive down the street and pull into a shopping mall parking lot, away from my neighborhood and anyone who might know me, before putting the company's corporate logo stickers on the front and rear windshields. This was my secret side gig, my double life, my incognito professional role.

Did I say how impressed I was with this company's app? Seriously, it made the process of getting riders in getting them around town seamless and smooth. Frankly, it almost gamified the experience, almost to the point where it was addictive. Driving into neighborhoods previously unknown became an adventure. I went down streets I had never heard of, and some I had heard of but had always avoided. I had people in the backseat of my car. We're obviously complete strangers, but suddenly they were depending on me to get them somewhere important safely, and I was depending on them to be trustworthy and respectful. Perhaps more so than any of my previous jobs, this role was risky, this role was challenging, this role was one I had to assume if I expected to pay the bills.

All blog posts in this chapter were written by Bob Cargill for the AMA Boston blog and are republished here with permission.

10 WAYS PUBLIC SPEAKERS SHOULD USE SOCIAL MEDIA

If you're giving a presentation and your audience members are looking down at their electronic devices, not up at you, don't be annoyed, be pleased.

As someone who speaks often at industry conferences and events, after all, I know that if those in my audience are looking down at their phones, tablets and laptops, they're probably not ignoring my presentation. They're likely sharing what they're hearing on social media, which is exactly what I want them to be doing on my behalf. I want them to be amplifying my message to their own networks, extending the reach of what I'm saying to a much larger number of people.

That's what I would call the "socialization" of my presentation. And that's what I would think every public speaker today would want their listeners to be doing for them, too. It may be disconcerting at first. It may even be distracting. But it's increasing the audience for your presentation exponentially. Like the click-click-click of the cameras at a big press conference, everyone is busy capturing the moment, only in a variety of different ways unique to each respective audience member.

Of course, a speaker wants everyone in the audience to be paying attention, hanging on his or her every word. But the reality is that when they're sharing what they hear with their own online followers and friends, they're concentrating even more on recording just the right sound bite or image. They're even more engaged with what you are saying as they realize the magnitude of their responsibility to report on the event accurately, informatively and entertainingly.

Here are 10 ways public speakers, instructors, trainers and anyone else who finds themselves in front of an audience should use social media to promote their own presentations...

1. Encourage social media use among your audience. *One of the first things I say to my audience when I take the stage is to not hesitate to use social media. After all, I want them to share their impressions of my presentation with their own respective networks. They get the benefit of having unique, new content to distribute and I enjoy the exponential increase in reach to a much broader audience. Its' a win-win situation that's well worth encouraging.*

2. Include your handle and hashtag in slides. *If you're going to be drumming up social media usage, it would be remiss of you not to include where you can be found there on your presentation's slides. At the very least, share your Twitter handle on your title slide and perhaps on every other slide, too. You should also list wherever else you have a presence on social media — e.g., YouTube, Instagram, LinkedIn, etc. — on an individual slide that also includes your bio, not to mention the event's hashtag (assuming there is one).*

3. Tweet before and after your presentation. *Publicizing your presentation nowadays means using social media to talk about it both beforehand and afterwards. Some of this content can be* scheduled in advance to give you a steady, uninterrupted presence on these online communications channels while the rest of it should be real-time engagement with your followers and fans.

4. Record your presentation. Have someone record your presentation on video, which will likely give you some great content afterwards to share — in dribs and drabs — with your constituents on social media. If the quality is good enough, you can even upload the entire presentation to YouTube.

5. Live-tweet your gig. Having someone capture what you're saying in the moment is an excellent way to report extemporaneously on your presentation, taking full advantage of any real-time buzz about your presentation and leveraging every little thing you are saying in the moment. Retweeting, liking and engaging with your audience is ideal, too, if you can get a colleague or friend to do this from their account for you while you're on stage.

6. Get away from the podium. Moving around the room is a good idea for a speaker in general, as it is a much more engaging and compelling way to deliver a presentation. You don't want your audience's view of you to be obstructed in any way, shape or form. You want to give them as many photo opportunities as possible as well as the best chance to see you up-close and personal. You'll make a stronger connection and better impression that way as well.

7. Include quotable quotes. Make it easy for members of your audience to provide coverage of your talk. Provide them with catchy visuals and short sound bites. Have a handful of clever, memorable one-liners rehearsed in advance and delivered at key, prominent moments. Feature this content prominently in your presentation. Create each of your slides for prime-time viewing, that is, with the intention of them going viral. Make it hard for your audience not to want to repeat what you share with them time and time again.

8. Pause on your best slides. *Pacing is important. If you have a hit slide or message on your hands, pause and pose for the crowd. Seriously. Take your time on the highlights of your presentation. Take it slow. Milk it for everything it's worth. If you have a strong point to make, or a great visual to show, your audience needs the time to capture and share the moment with their own respective audiences on social media.*

9. Use gestures and props. *You may be speaking to inform and educate, but you also want to entertain your audience. Accessorize your presentation with gestures and props. Not only do you want to engage and enlighten those in the audience, you want to dazzle and delight them, too. Appeal to their senses. Tease them with theatrics. Add elements to your presentation that will make it more photogenic, capturable and ripe for social media.*

10. Summarize your presentation. *When all is said and done, you want to review, repurpose and save your presentation for posterity. You want to summarize it for those who weren't there as much as get even more mileage out of your efforts by reporting on it yourself. Use Storify, Twitter Moments or your own blog to recapture everything you said as well as what your audience had to say themselves on social media about the event.*

Note: This post, "10 Ways Public Speakers Should Use Social Media," was originally published on the AMA Boston blog on September 7, 2017, and is republished here with permission.

10 THINGS WRONG WITH MARKETING TODAY

I have met the enemy and it is us.

Yup. Not to sound like an alarmist, but if those of us who earn our livelihoods in marketing continue down the same long, circuitous path we've been on since the turn of this millennium, we may as well throw our hands up in the air and cry "uncle."

Never mind the Joneses, after all, we're hardly keeping up with anyone anymore on the receiving end of our marketing messages.

We're moving in circles as an industry, if we're moving at all. We're falling dangerously far behind.

We need to wake up and smell the cold-brewed coffee. We need to stop marketing like it's 1999 and start realizing that it's no longer business as usual.

This is 2017 going on a future like you and I can only begin to imagine. This is no time to hem and haw.

Please don't shoot the messenger, either. I'm merely passing along these words to the wise not just based on my own hands-on experience, but on what I've been hearing through the grapevine lately.

As disconcerting as it may be to digest, here are 10 things that are wrong with marketing today...

1. Spam. *What junk mail did to direct mail, spam has done to email. People are receiving far too many irrelevant emails from brands they don't want to hear from, undermining the effectiveness of those online messages of ours that are targeted and timed so well. You know what they about a few bad apples. Read "Why Do Marketers in 2017 Still Spam?"*

2. Trust. *Ask around. Where do you think those of us in marketing and advertising stand in the minds of consumers? Down there with lobbyists, politicians, telemarketers and car salespeople. Ouch. Read "Attention Marketers! People Don't Trust Your Marketing Strategy!"*

3. Innovation. *Ironic, isn't it? Innovate is what we do day in and day out, yet we're still not doing it quickly enough. Read "Nick*

245

*Law: There's a Lack of Imagination in the Advertising Industry"
You can read this article here... https://www.adnews.com.au/
news/nick-law-there-s-a-lack-of-imagination-in-the-adver-
tising-industry*

4. Knowledge. *We may be smart, but our knowledge as individual practitioners still pales in comparison to what members
of our audience know collectively. They're a diverse, dynamic
group, constantly in motion, perpetually changing. A culture of
continuous learning within the marketing workplace must be a
top priority going forward. Read "Marketers Lack the Skills to
Deliver on Customer Experience" You can read this article here...
https://www.emarketer.com/Article/Marketers-Lack-Skills-De-
liver-on-Customer-Experience/1014169*

5. Technology. *Ah, the bane of our existence. As soon as we
catch on to one disruptive trend, another one comes along.
Yikes. More changes in technology have taken place in the
21st century than most, if not all of us, have seen in our life-
times. Read "Staying Technology Relevant Has Suddenly
Become a Full-Time Responsibility" You can read this article
here... https://www.forbes.com/sites/larryalton/2016/10/21/
staying-technologically-relevant-has-suddenly-be-
come-a-full-time-responsibility/?sh=5b309b2965b4*

6. Agencies. *This one hurts personally, as agencies have been
the lifeblood of my career. But all good things must come to an
end, and the agency model as we know it needs to undergo a
massive overhaul if you, me and everyone else in this industry
expects to thrive, not just survive as professionals. Read Forrest-
er: Marketers are the Catalyst to Fix the Broken Agency Model
and Marketing agencies are broken. You can read these articles
here... https://www.adexchanger.com/agencies/forrester-mar-
keters-catalyst-fix-broken-agency-model/ and here... https://
venturebeat.com/2016/07/04/marketing-agencies-are-broken/*

7. Quality. *We can't say we didn't see this coming. Unfortunately, what our parents warned us about while growing up has finally come true. Call it carelessness. Call it informality. Call it inattention to grammar, punctuation, detail and accuracy. Whatever we call it, it could cost us our jobs. Read "Poor-Quality Ads Cost U.S. Marketers $7.4 Billion" You can read this article here... https://www.mediapost.com/publications/article/298526/poor-quality-ads-cost-us-marketers-74-billion.html*

8. Turnover. *A lack of continuity and cohesion among teams, especially those at the leadership level, is never good for business. So-called churn-and-burn hiring may never end, but it needs to at least slow down for not just the agency era, but for the marketing industry as we know it to endure. Read "CMO Turnover Reaches New High" You can read this article here... https://www.forbes.com/sites/johnellett/2016/08/02/cmo-turnover-reaches-new-high/?sh=7461fa231a15*

9. Strategy. *Why do you think so many ads are being blocked, ignored and avoided today? Why do you think consumers have turned against us? We're not putting enough time, effort and thought into what we do, that's why. We're sacrificing strategy for expediency. We're cutting corners to cut costs. We're being penny wise and pound foolish. Read "10 Reasons You Need a Digital Marketing Strategy in 2017" You can read this article here... https://www.smartinsights.com/digital-marketing-strategy/digital-strategy-development/10-reasons-for-digital-marketing-strategy/*

10. Irrelevancy. *Not to sound like a broken record, but we need to do for ourselves what we do for our products, services, clients and customers. We can't be like the cobbler and his shoes. We need to not just rebrand ourselves, but literally transform ourselves from the inside out before it's too late. Read "5 of the Biggest Challenges Facing Today's Marketers"*

All that said, this is a fantastically fun time to be in marketing. Seriously. We just need a big course correction, that's all. We need to seize the day. Digital. Mobile. Social. AI. Augmented reality. Chat bots. Ephemeral content. Livestreaming video. You name it. There are more opportunities than ever today to take our industry further and faster than we ever could have imagined. I absolutely love my job. I love what I do for a living. I love a good challenge. Who else is in?

Note: This post, "10 Things Wrong with Marketing Today," was originally published on the AMA Boston blog on October 10, 2017, and is republished here with permission.

The following posts were written by Bob Cargill and originally appeared with accompanying videos on either his Instagram or YouTube accounts.

DON'T TELL ME YOU DON'T HAVE TIME FOR SOCIAL MEDIA.

by Bob Cargill on Instagram on February 9, 2020.

Either you don't know how to use it, you don't like it, or you don't believe in it.

That's probably more like it.

If you don't make time for social media in 2020, however, you may fall dangerously behind your competition, not to mention your friends and your family.

From athletes to politicians, marketers to advertisers, educators to entertainers grandparents to distant relatives, people of all ages, in all walks of life, are using social media nowadays to communicate and stay in touch.

Social media is an extension of who you are as not just a professional, but as a human being.

Social media gives you the opportunity to show that you have a personality, not just a pulse.

Social media can be good for your career and your business, your health and your confidence.

Social media can be done on the fly, too. It doesn't have to be choreographed, scheduled and automated.

It doesn't have to be perfect.

Some of the best social media activities are impromptu and extemporaneous, done manually by real people in real time, authentically and transparently, flaws and all.

Whatever you do, wherever you are, if you want to communicate effectively, don't overlook the importance of social media.

by Bob Cargill on Instagram on March 6, 2020.

In the last 15 years or so, #SocialMedia has been a major disruption to how we #communicate with one another in both our professional and personal lives.

About 70% of adults in the United States are using #Facebook today.

#LinkedIn has over 600 million members.

More than 100 million people are using #Instagram.

Something like five billion videos are watched on #YouTube daily.

There are #blogs and #podcasts, #TikTok and #Snapchat.

There are more resources for education, entertainment and enrichment than ever available to us instantaneously and inexpensively.

This is how we learn. This is how we listen.

This is how we get things done. This is how we pass our time.

People hardly ever the answer their landlines anymore.

Newspapers and magazines are falling by the wayside.

Almost everyone has a smartphone in their hands.

We go to Twitter for breaking news and hilarious memes.

We create stories of our lives and share them instantaneously with the world.

We're connected online in way or another practically all the time.

Never mind #marketing, the field in which I earn my livelihood, #business in general has undergone a digital transformation.

The art of #communications has changed completely in the last decade or two.

Have you and your business kept up with the times?

▌ COME DOWN FROM YOUR IVORY TOWERS.

Written by Bob Cargill on YouTube on October 29, 2020.

Come down from your ivory towers. That was a big takeaway for me after reading the book, The Cluetrain Manifesto, back in the day.

That point was made loud and clear to me.

Business executives needed to stop distancing themselves from their constituents and instead start talking to them and even more importantly, listening to them on the internet.

It's been some 20 years since this book was published, but its main message holds true now more than ever.

Thanks to social media, there is no excuse anymore not to be engaging with your customers, prospects, connections, followers, subscribers, fans and even critics.

The savviest and smartest marketers and advertisers get it. They're conspicuous in their presence online day in and day out. They're joining the conversations on LinkedIn, Twitter, Facebook, Instagram and the like, if not leading them. They're strengthening their reputations, supporting their networks, building trust, developing relationships and generating leads.

They've come down from their ivory towers and they'll never look back.

IF I WERE A BUSINESS OR BRAND WITH THE BUDGET

Written by Bob Cargill on YouTube on October 27, 2021.

If I were a business or a brand with the budget, I would hire people whose sole responsibility was to use social media on my behalf.

They would cover everything that's going on behind the scenes, sharing content day in and day out with our audience of fans, followers and friends.

The content they create and share would be educational, informative, insightful, supportive, inspirational, entertaining even.

They would be conspicuous in their presence, responsive and engaging, friendly and dependable.

They would interact with those on the receiving end of our messages and learn from them.

They would be a better and more successful company in the long run because of this commitment to #SocialMedia.

 ## PUTTING YOURSELF OUT THERE ON SOCIAL MEDIA

Written by Bob Cargill on YouTube on December 16, 2021.

Unless you're a big brand or a celebrity, to be effective on social media means to put yourself out there.

That's the SOCIAL in social media.

You have to be willing and able to share content frequently that is educational, enlightening, entertaining even.

You have to show the personal side of what you do for a living, not just the professional side, giving people a look behind the scenes, helping those on the receiving end of your messages get to know you and your colleagues as fellow human beings.

The more your audience gets to know you on #SocialMedia, the more likely they'll be to do business with you when the opportunities arise.

 ## MAKE TIME FOR SOCIAL MEDIA

Written by Bob Cargill on YouTube on February 1, 2022.

I hear it all the time.

I don't have time for social media.

Yet social media doesn't have to take much time at all.

Spend a few minutes here and a few minutes there.

Share what you're doing. Share what you're thinking.

Like someone else's content. Comment on that content.

A little time on social media goes a long way toward establishing your online presence, building your brand and making people aware that you are open for business.

A little time spent on social media is time well spent.

Written by Bob Cargill on YouTube on April 20, 2022.

You have a long road ahead of you.

Take it one step at a time.

Take care of yourself.

Believe in yourself.

Push through adversity.

Don't let anything get in your way.

Don't let anyone question the direction in which you are heading.

It's all about the journey, not the destination.

But yes, when all is said and done, you will cross that finish line a winner.

Written by Bob Cargill on YouTube on March 16, 2022.

A lot of people tend to give up right before they're about to win.

They've exerted themselves.

They've exhausted themselves.

And they're not sure that they have anything left in themselves.

Don't make that mistake.

You can do it.

Believe in yourself.

Keep on keeping on.

I have been recording many videos the last few years that I share on social media. Some are about marketing and social media. Others are motivational, which I tell people are as much for myself as they are for my audience. I need the positive self-talk as much as anybody else.

CONCLUSION

It took me about 16 months to write the first draft of this book and even longer to have it edited, designed, vetted and published. This book has been well over three years in the making. While I was working on it, I told a lot of people about it, and after saying congratulations to me, almost all of them asked me why I was writing it. That was a good question.

First of all, writers write. It's in my blood. It's in my head. It's what I know. It's what I do.

I chronicle things for a living. How can I not chronicle my own professional life?

But I've done so for other reasons besides simply wanting documentation of my career so far.

I wrote this book for you. I want to entertain and educate you, as well as prepare and even inspire you.

I want to teach you a few lessons that I learned the hard way. I want you to realize that almost all is fair in the business world. It is a rough and tumble professional existence, one that if I could do it all over again, I might not choose.

Life is a series of trade-offs, some good, some not so much. However, I have made the most of my career so far. There have been many highlights and experiences that I wouldn't give up for anything.

I want to show you that almost anything's possible if you are determined and perseverent. While I didn't see myself at a young age eventually writing direct mail for a living, or tens of thousands of tweets, I did envision myself writing, period.

I don't know exactly why I never stayed at one company for more than a few years when I worked full-time in the business world.

In a way, maybe it was a case of me getting the yips, being anxious about what would happen if I remained at a certain place so long and was forced to experience something I had never experienced before, tenure. What would that be like? How would I feel being a veteran of one company?

When a dog chases a car, what does he do when he catches it?

Perhaps I was overly careful about what I wished for.

I was always comfortable starting over, that's for sure. That's what I knew, that's what I did. I started over and over and over again.

Despite the long and winding road I have traveled, though, I have found a way to keep my hands on the wheel and my eyes focused on the many different directions I have wanted to go, not necessarily the ones others have given me along the way.

Frankly, I don't think I've reached my destination yet. I certainly hope not. I hope, as Robert Frost once wrote, "I have miles to go before I sleep."

EPILOGUE

I left my last full-time job in the spring of 2017, and I haven't looked back. Wait a minute, that's not true. I did look back, all the way back to 1983...in writing this book over the course of the last three-plus years.

But seriously, after all those years plying my trade in the corporate world as a copywriter, creative director, social media director and other related titles, I decided to take advantage of the gig economy and commit myself to working solely as a freelancer, contractor, consultant and adjunct professor, the latter taking up the bulk of my professional time these days. In fact, I can't tell you how much I enjoy teaching marketing and social media to college students at not one, not two, but three different universities in Boston. I am so elated to be working in the field of higher education, it makes me wish I discovered this calling much earlier in my career. Better late than never, though. Right?

I realize how fortunate I am to have been so successful in marketing all these years, even though I constantly compare myself to those who have made millions of dollars and have attained senior business executive ranks as opposed to creative craftspeople like me, those who are lucky to have simply worked in the industry and have even a modicum of savings in the bank as a result.

Perspective, empathy and understanding how others live, work and play is so important in life. We shouldn't take anything for granted.

Everything happens for a reason, I often think. Here I am now working more hours and earning less money than at any other stage of my career, yet my level of job satisfaction is greater than ever. Much greater.

Yes, I couldn't be happier today as a professional, especially having found the time to finally write a book.

Yay, me. And yay, you, for taking an interest in reading that book. I hope you've not only learned a lot from it, but that you've been both enlightened and entertained.

Please don't hesitate to provide me with your feedback, by the way. Write a review of this book. Tell others about it. Shout from the rooftops whatever you think about it. Reach out to me on social media if we aren't already connected there, too. Stay in touch. Take care of yourself. And as my own Lesson 5 says, believe in yourself. Always.

Here's proof that I always wanted to be a writer, even if it meant standing on a kitchen chair to tap the keys of a manual typewriter as a toddler.

AUTHOR

Bob Cargill, who was the New England Direct Marketing Association's Direct Marketer of the Year in 2009, is an adjunct professor, a copywriter, content creator, social media consultant and public speaker who has worked for some 500 or so different clients over the years.

His work has been recognized with over 40 awards from the New England Direct Marketing Association, including Gold for his blog on marketing, Gold for Best Tweets, Silver for Best Copywriting and two Silvers for his video series about social media on LinkedIn.

Bob is a past president of both the American Marketing Association Boston (fiscal years 2018-2020) and the New England Direct Marketing Association (fiscal year 1999-2000). In addition to hosting his own podcast on marketing and recording YouTube videos about social media on a weekly basis, Bob also contributes regularly to his blog at thebobcargill.com that he began writing in 2004. Bob resides in the suburbs west of Boston with his wife, Barbara, with whom he shares two sons, Scott and Ben, and two stepchildren, David and Sophie.

EDITOR

Morgan Hume is a communications professional with experience in news writing and public relations. She graduated from Suffolk University in 2020 with a degree in journalism. When she steps away from the computer, you can find her crocheting, reading or sipping on (too much) coffee. Morgan is from Troy, New York and currently lives in the Greater Boston area. **(Photo by: Haley Clegg Photography)**

GRAPHIC DESIGNER

Maria Antonia Silva is a UX designer and web developer consultant. She graduated from Suffolk University in 2021 with a degree in computer science and graphic design. When she is not with clients she spends her time playing piano in a local band, working out at the gym or spending hours at the movies. Maria Antonia lives in the town she grew up, Shrewsbury, Massachusetts.

Please don't hesitate to reach out to Bob Cargill, the author of Twenty Jobs, Twenty Lessons — a Long, Strange Career in Marketing, from Junk Mail to Social Media, anytime, at Cargill123@gmail.com. His website is located at thebobcargill.com. You can find and follow him almost anywhere on social media as well, as you will see below.

Podcast: www.bobcargill.podbean.com

LinkedIn: www.linkedin.com/in/bobcargill

Twitter: www.twitter.com/thebobcargill

Facebook: www.facebook.com/thebobcargill

YouTube: www.youtube.com/bobcargill

Instagram: www.instagram.com/bobcargill

TikTok: www.tiktok.com/@thebobcargill

Pinterest: www.pinterest.com/bobcargill

Made in the USA
Coppell, TX
23 June 2022

79132670R10149